MILLION DOLLAR GAME

by
DAVID DIPOALI

Without limiting the rights under the copyright reserved above, no part of this publication may be produced or transmitted in any form or by any means, whether electronical, mechanical photocopying, recording, storage retrieval systems, and or by any other means known, unknown and or created in the future, without the prior written consent of the publisher of this book.

Copyright © 2014 by Kaleidoscopic Publishing. All Rights Reserved.
ISBN - 978-0-9903853-0-1 (print)
ISBN - 978-0-9903853-1-8 (e-book)
ISBN - 978-0-9903853-2-5 (Mobi)
First published in 2014 by Kaleidoscopic Publishing
First Printing on November 1, 2014
Printed in The United States

Library of Congress Cataloging-in-publication data
The name Kaleidoscopic and its symbol are trademarks of Kaleidoscopic Publishing

If you suspect that an unauthorized vendor or person is selling or distributing this publication, please contact us at www.kaleidoscopicpublishing.com You could be entitled to an award and remain anonymous for your reporting. This also applies to unauthorized copying and distributing.

CONTENTS

COPYRIGHTS 8

- COPYRIGHTS 8
- FIXED FORM 8
- WHAT CAN BE COPYRIGHTED 8
- WHAT IS NOT COPYRIGHTABLE 8
- COPYRIGHT NOTICE 10
- SOUND RECORDING NOTICE 10
- UNPUBLISHED NOTICES/SYMBOLS 11
- PENDING COPYRIGHT 11
- COPYRIGHT OWNERSHIP TERMS 11
- PSEUDONYMOUS 11
- AUTHOR'S SIGNATURE 12
- COPYRIGHT BOARD 12
- INFRINGEMENT FEES 13
- TYPES OF COPYRIGHT FORMS THAT EXIST 13
- COPYRIGHT FEES 14
- COPYRIGHT ADDRESS 14
- COPYRIGHT FORMS 15

TRADEMARKS 39

- SERVICE MARKS 40
- INFRINGEMENT FEES 41
- DURATION OF TRADEMARK/SERVICE MARK 41
- ESTABLISHING FIRST USE 41
- POOR MAN'S PROOF 42
- TRADEMARK & SERVICE MARK FEES 42
- AMENDMENTS & ADDITIONAL FEES 43
- LIST OF GOODS 43
- HOW TO SECURE YOUR OWN TRADEMARK/SERVICE MARK 43
- MOTION MARKS 45
- DIGITAL IMAGES 45
- PAPER SIZE 46
- SPECIMEN 46
- TRADEMARK INFRINGEMENT FEES 47
- CLASSIFICATION OF GOODS AND SERVICES CODES ... 47

STATE TRADEMARKS	*54*
STATE TRADEMARK/SERVICE MARK FORMS	*54*

PATENTS **68**

PATENTS	*68*
OVERVIEW	*70*

DOMAIN NAMES **71**

DOMAIN NAMES	*71*
ONCE DOMAIN NAME IS PROCURED	*74*
SECURITY BADGE	*74*
HOW TO OBTAIN A DOMAIN NAME	*74*

CORPORATIONS **76**

ADDRESSES & WEBSITES FOR DIFFERENT STATES	*76*
CONVICTED FELONS	*86*
TYPES OF CORPORATIONS	*87*
SIMPLICITY OF CORPORATE ESTABLISHING	*88*
THE DIFFERENCE BETWEEN LLC & C CORPORATION	*90*
DIRECTORS	*93*
EMPLOYEE ISSUES	*95*
EMPLOYEES OR INDEPENDENT CONTRACTORS	*95*
EMPLOYEE AGREEMENT	*96*
EMPLOYEE LAWS	*96*
EMPLOYEE BENEFITS	*97*
HOW TO INCORPORATE	*98*
COVER LETTER OF A C CORPORATION	*98*
LLC FORM	*99*
C CORPORATION FORM	*101*
CORPORATE BANK RESOLUTION	*111*
AFTER INCORPORATING	*112*
FICTITIOUS NAMES	*115*
FICTITIOUS NAME FORMS	*118*

BE YOUR OWN CEO OR GENERAL MANAGER AND RUN YOUR OWN COMPANY AND OR CORPORATION **119**

RUN YOUR OWN COMPANY AND OR CORPORATION	*119*
VISION	*120*
RECRUIT PEOPLE SMARTER THAN YOU	*120*

A POWERHOUSE MANAGEMENT TEAM	*120*
NETWORK	*120*
GLOBALIZE	*121*
CHECKINGS AND SAVINGS ACCOUNT	*121*
PAY FOR NOTHING IN CASH	*121*
MENTOR TO THE NEXT GENERATION OF YOUR SEEDS	*121*
DEVELOP AN EXIT STRATEGY	*122*

REGISTERING WITH DUN & BRADSTREET 123

DUN & BRADSTREET	*123*
DUN & BRADSTREET REGISTRATION FORM	*125*

SECURING BUSINESS CREDIT 134

BUSINESS CREDIT	*134*
PAYDEX SCORE	*135*
RATING	*135*
REFERENCES	*136*
SHORTCUT TO BUSINESS CREDIT	*137*

FIXING YOUR OWN CREDIT & EXCLUDING CREDIT REPAIRERS 142

FIXING YOUR CREDIT & EXCLUDING CREDIT REPAIRERS	*142*
ANNUAL CREDIT REPORT REQUEST FORM	*146*
CREDIT AGENCY LETTER	*147*
CREDIT DISCREPANCIES LETTER	*148*

FAMILIARIZING YOURSELF WITH UCC 149

UNIFORM COMMERCIAL CODE (UCC)	*149*
UCC-1 FINANCIAL STATEMENT FORM	*152*
UCC-3 FINANCIAL STATEMENT AMENDMENT FORM	*153*
UCC-1 FINANCIAL STATEMENT INSTRUCTIONS	*154*
UCC-3 FINANCIAL STATEMENT AMENDMENT INSTRUCTIONS	*156*

ASSIGNING YOUR BUSINESS A SOLID ASSET 160

FORMING SOLID BUSINESS ASSETS	*160*

SECURING BUSINESS LOANS 163

SECURING A BUSINESS LOAN	*163*
APOSTILLE LETTER	*167*
RECORDS AND REGISTRATION LETTER	*168*

UCC-1 FINANCIAL STATEMENT EXAMPLE... *169*
PROMISSORY NOTE... *170*
UCC-1 SECURITY AGREEMENT... *171*
LOAN SATISFICATION CERTIFICATION FORM... *185*

UNTAPPED COMMERCIAL ACCOUNTS... *190*

USING YOUR OWN MONEY AS LEVERAGE *192*

LEGALLY CHANGE YOUR NAME TO A NAME THAT EXHUDES MONEY, POWER AND RESPECT.. *193*
NAME CHANGE MOTION.. *193*

BURYING NEGATIVE INFORMATION ABOUT YOU ON GOOGLE.......... *198*
CONCLUSION.. *200*

LIMIT OF LIABILITY/DISCLAIMER OF WARRANTY

While the publisher and author have used their best efforts in preparing this book, they make no representations or warranties with respect to the accuracy or completeness of it; and specifically disclaim any implied warranties of merchantability or fitness for a particular purpose. No warranty may be created or extended by sales representatives or written sales materials. The advice and strategies contained herein may not be suitable for your situation. The publisher nor author is not engaged in rendering professional services, and you should consult a professional where professional advice is needed. Neither the publisher nor author shall be liable for any loss or profit or any other commercial damages, including but not limited to special, incidental, consequential, or other.

In addition, the Representations in this book change over time; and by necessity of the lapse in time between the writing and printing hereof, may possibly be out of date upon the First publication. Therefore, each reader must use caution in applying any material contained herein.

I'm also not an attorney; financial, securities, investment, nor credit advisor/consultant, etc. and am not providing you such advice per se, on any of these matters, included but not limited to taxes, etc.; and where such credentials are required, such credentials must be sought; and the Author and publisher of this book am 'exempt' from any faults, liabilities, and or suits as a result.

Nothing within this book is a scheme or scam, it is real and if applied lawfully and correctly, could reap you lucrative benefits. Why am I giving up the ghosts? Because I can get paid more for sharing it with the world. Like they say, the game is to be sold....not told.

enjoy,

CHAPTER 1

COPYRIGHTS

COPYRIGHTS

Copyrights is a form of protection provided by the laws of the United States that protects literary, dramatic, musical, artistic and certain other intellectual works. The protection is available to both published **and non published** works, from the time the work is created in fixed form.

FIXED FORM

A 'fixed form' (which is also known as a tangible form of expression) is defined by being able to be communicated with the aide of a machine or device.

WHAT CAN BE COPYRIGHTED?

Any literary (written) work, musical works (including accompanying words), dramatic works (including any accompanying music), pantomimes and choreography works, pictorial, graphic and sculptural works, motion pictures and any other audiovisual works, sound recordings, architectural works etc. Every type of copyright falls within one of these categories.

WHAT IS NOT COPYRIGHTABLE?

The following things are not copyrightable, titles, names, short phrases, slogans, familiar symbols or designs, mere variations of typographic ornamentation, lettering, coloring, mere listings of ingredients or contents, ideas, procedures, methods, systems, processes, days, dates, years, measurements, tables and etc.

There is however, one rule to circumvent this, which no one else will share with you if they knew of it. It is that you copyright all of the above if you referred it to something specific.

For Example: say you're trying to copyright a symbol, in referenced to a distinguished mark regarding a record label. On the copyright form, under the 'Nature of Authorship" section (2(a)) states: briefly describe nature of material created by this author in which copyright is claimed. You will then provide: see additional page attached. On the additional page attached you will list a drawing of the symbol and state underneath: For use as a distinct business symbol in the entertainment field.

What you have done is secured copyright protection for that mark, in that no one in the entertainment field can use it without your prior permission and or compensation.

Another Example: Say you had an idea about marketing a water brand, and the idea was surrounded by the name 'wonder water.' Under the nature of authorship section you would state: see additional page attached. On the additional page attached you will list" 'Wonder Water" and then state underneath: 'a specific business title regarding a liquid product for human consumption.' Accordingly, you have prohibited anyone else from using the name 'Wonder Water.'

One More Example: Say I thought of a good artist name, figuring it'll someday make me millions of dollars. The name is 'Justify.' Under the nature of authorship section you would state: see additional page attached. On the additional page attached you will list: 'Justify' then state underneath: regarding the specific name of a male artist in the entertainment field. Wherefore, you have prohibited anyone in the music industry from publicly using the name 'Justify' as an artists or entertainer.

You should understand where I'm coming from by now. Be clear, precise, direct and specific when copyrighting.

The biggest myth regarding copyrighting is that copyrighting automatically grants the copywriter ownership to the copyrighted work. This is far from the intentions of the copyright's office. So while it may be true that copyrighting your work affords you protection under the copyright laws, it does not however, grant you automatic ownership to such works you submit.

What copyright protection affords is the privilege to have your work copyrighted in the Library of Congress, thereby having your work registered with an accredited archive storer. Automatic ownership boils down to "FIRST USE." The intentions of the Library of Congress was that if your work was filed with them and someone appeared later claiming ownership then it could be proven that you were in fact the first owner on record. So while it is in fact true that nothing is new under the sun, ownership of such property(s) is established via the provided evidence of first use. What that means is that you could have a registered work with the Library of Congress, regarding the date of today. And you thereafter further invest into that work and make it a global brand. Only to find out that someone else has established and used this work five years ago. Guess whom it belongs to? If you guessed that you were shit out of luck then you were right. So no matter what, establish first use and then get your work registered.

COPYRIGHT NOTICE

If your work have never before been published then you must have a notice/symbol (C) followed by the year, and then followed by the copyright owner's full name. This identifies that your work is copyrighted and such identity places the world on notice of such.

Example: (c)2013 John James
This notice should initially be listed on the "Cover Page" of your work, and additionally on the bottom of every page there afterwards.

SOUND RECORDING NOTICE

If your work consists of a sound recording (in its literary form) then you must have a sound recording protection notice/symbol (P) listed, followed by the year, and then followed by the copyright owner's full name. Such notice identifies and protects your work as indicated above.

Example: (P) 2013 John James
This notice should initially be listed on the cover page of your work, and additionally on the bottom of every page there afterwards as well.

UNPUBLISHED NOTICES/SYMBOLS

If you have unpublished works or sound recordings, then you must place the world on notice that such work is protected under ownership of the copyright claimant/author/owner. Such notice must be followed by the following example:
    Unpublished Work (C)2013 John James
    Unpublished Work (P)2013 John James Entertainment, Inc.

PENDING COPYRIGHT

If you have work pending copyright then you must inform the world of such. Such notice must be followed by the following examples:
    Pending Copyright (C)2013 John James
    Pending Copyright (P)2013 John James Entertainment, Inc.

COPYRIGHT OWNERSHIP TERMS

If you are the rightful owner of said copyrighted work, then such ownership is automatically protected from the moment of its creation in fixed form, until the death of the author/owner, plus seventy (70) years after the author/owner's death. So be mindful of the date you establish your copyright; but be surely mindful to first secure the establishment of such date.

PSEUDONYMOUS

Pseudonymous is a form of hidden identity on the copyright form wherein its authors do not want the public to know their relationship or connection with the work or the work's views. People usually use pseudonymous for a variety of other reasons as well. Say an author may be well known for writing 'law works.' Well he may be the author of works in other fields as well, that may not coincide with people knowing about his works of law.

Say for example he is also well versed in the field of children works. His audience in the law field would probably not imagine him in the field of children works, so what he does is list the author of copyright in the children work field in a fictitious name, usually a name that he or she will probably make up, or a name that sounds well attractive for an artist in the field of children book writing. for example: Mr. Magoo, by Mary Poppins.

Listing a pseudonymous is very common in such fields. People write biographies on themselves all the time and list the author of copyright in another name to avoid the public being aware of them stroking their own egos. Bottom line is, pseudonymous is used for many reasons and for good cause. On the copyright form under section 2(a) there's a part on the right hand section of the form that states: "was the author's contribution to this work anonymous or pseudonymous?" If you check pseudonymous be sure to list on both pages of the form, where it regards "Name of Author," your government name and your pseudonymous. An example is as followed:

John James whose Pseudonymous is J.J. Fad.

AUTHOR'S SIGNATURE

On every line that requires the author's signature, be sure to implicate the author's social security number besides him or her name. This is not necessary but helps to pin point the exact author responsible for the work.
The form requires only the author's name and year of birth. However, contemplate the number of identical names that was born in the exact year you were born. Then contemplate your loved ones sifting through various databases in an attempt to determine what property rightfully belongs to you – after your death.

It would make matters much easier to document your social security number next to your full name, wherein it'll be easier to locate what's yours and what's to be left to your kids inheritance regarding financial support.

COPYRIGHT BOARD

The Department of the Copyright Office that set certain fees for authorised uses of copyrighted material implemented the Copyright Board. This board set price fees to the public for use of an author's copyrighted material. This means that everytime your work is used you're entitled to a minimum fee set. To learn more about these fees and how they work, visit: http://www.loc.gov/crb/
Don't look for anyone to tell you about this board. Then again, don't look for anyone else to tell you many of the things you'll get out of this book.

INFRINGEMENT FEES

Copyrights are serious matters, and infringers pay out huge settlements. Pursuant to 17 U.S.C. §504(c)(1), a court will award no less than $750 dollars, but no more than $30,000 dollars per act, to an author/owner of copyright, when his or her copyright has been infringed upon.
Pursuant to 17 U.S.C. §504(c), the court may, in a further discretion, award as much as $150,000 per act of infringement if it finds willfulness.

TYPE OF COPYRIGHT FORMS THAT EXIST

There are several types of copyright forms that exists. In utilizing them, each have their own purpose for its aforementioned classes. The common ones however are PA, SE, SB, VA, and TX.
Followed are its various types and specific uses:

PA: This form is a registration form for works of the performing arts, which consists of musical and dramatic works, pantomimes and choreographic works, motion pictures and other works.
These forms are used to copyright any works that is to be performed before an audience, whether tv, radio and or any other type of transmittance assistance. I usually use these forms for plays, screenplays, sitcom and commercial literary scripts, scripted theatrics, comedy scripts, etc. However, your imagination is your limit.
SE: For serials, works issued or intended to be used in successive parts bearing numerical or chronological designations and intended to be continued indefinitely. For example, periodicals, newspapers, magazines, newsletters, annuals, journals, etc.
SR: This is a sound recording registration form. Its use is self explanatory; and used in conjunction with certain sounds. A copy of the sound (whether via tape, cassette, dvd, etc.) is to be submitted with the registration form to The Library of Congress when copyrighting.
VA: Visual Arts is a registration form dealing with visual performances. As with the SR Form, said visual performances must be recorded and submitted as a specimen to The Library of Congress when applying for a copyright. Often, visual arts registrations are often submitted under pictorials,

graphics, sculptural and architectural works. I myself usually utilize these forms for my personal pictures, graphic designs etc.

TX: This form is for non dramatic literary works. An example is regarding a register of things in its creative ways, in which I spoke of earlier in the "what is not protected" section. Specific addressing to your names, ideas, slogans, descriptions, etc. and whatever else your mind can lead you on the path to imagining, is protectable.

FORM CA: This form is for supplementary registration to correct or amplify information given in the copyright office record of an earlier registration.

GR/CP: This is an adjunct application to be used for registration of a group of contributions to periodicals in addition to an application for TX, PA or VA.

COPYRIGHT FEES

As of the writing of this hook, all copyrighting fees varied. But the average fee per form was $65 dollars in U.S. currency, paid by United States Postal money order and credit cards only (no cash, cashiers and nor personal checks).

COPYRIGHT ADDRESS

To register your work, secure the necessary copyright forms from www.copyright.gov.com or call (202)707-3000. You can be given the correct fee for each specific form if asked. After filling out the form(s), mail the registration, along with the correct amount, to:

LIBRARY OF CONGRESS
COPYRIGHT OFFICE
101 INDEPENDENCE AVE., SE
WASHINGTON, D.C. 20559-6000

or complete the entire process online.

Below, are all the copyright forms you may need to secure ownership of your protected works. I have intentionally decided however, to exclude group protection forms for reasons that groups rarely apply for copyrights unless they're family. Again, the group registration forms are GR/CP applications which can be obtained online at the above stated online address.

Form PA

Detach and read these instructions before completing this form.
Make sure all applicable spaces have been filled in before you return this form.

BASIC INFORMATION

When to Use This Form: Use Form PA for registration of published or unpublished works of the performing arts. This class includes works prepared for the purpose of being "performed" directly before an audience or indirectly "by means of any device or process." Works of the performing arts include: (1) musical works, including any accompanying words; (2) dramatic works, including any accompanying music; (3) pantomimes and choreographic works; and (4) motion pictures and other audiovisual works.

Deposit to Accompany Application: An application for copyright registration must be accompanied by a deposit consisting of copies or phonorecords representing the entire work for which registration is made. The following are the general deposit requirements as set forth in the statute:

Unpublished Work: Deposit one complete copy (or phonorecord).

Published Work: Deposit two complete copies (or one phonorecord) of the best edition.

Work First Published Outside the United States: Deposit one complete copy (or phonorecord) of the first foreign edition.

Contribution to a Collective Work: Deposit one complete copy (or phonorecord) of the best edition of the collective work.

Motion Pictures: Deposit *both* of the following: (1) a separate written description of the contents of the motion picture; and (2) for a published work, one complete copy of the best edition of the motion picture; or, for an unpublished work, one complete copy of the motion picture or identifying material. Identifying material may be either an audiorecording of the entire soundtrack or one frame enlargement or similar visual print from each 10-minute segment.

The Copyright Notice: Before March 1, 1989, the use of copyright notice was mandatory on all published works, and any work first published before that date should have carried a notice. For works first published on and after March 1, 1989, use of the copyright notice is optional. For more information about copyright notice, see Circular 3, *Copyright Notice*.

For Further Information: To speak to a Copyright Office staff member, call (202) 707-3000 (TTY: (202) 707-6737). Recorded information is available 24 hours a day. Order forms and other publications from the address in space 9 or call the Forms and Publications Hotline at (202) 707-9100. Access and download circulars, forms, and other information from the Copyright Office website at *www.copyright.gov*.

> **PRIVACY ACT ADVISORY STATEMENT Required by the Privacy Act of 1974 (P.L. 93-579)**
>
> The authority for requesting this information is title 17 *USC* secs. 409 and 410. Furnishing the requested information is voluntary. But if the information is not furnished, It may be necessary to delay or refuse registration and you may not be entitled to certain relief, remedies, and benefits provided in chapters 4 and 5 of title 17 *USC*.
>
> The principal uses of the requested Information are the establishment and maintenance of a public record and the examination of the application for compliance with the registration requirements of the copyright code.
>
> Other routine uses Include public inspection and copying, preparation of public indexes, preparation of public catalogs of copyright registrations, and preparation of search reports upon request.
>
> **NOTE:** No other advisory statement will be given In connection with this application. Please keep this statement and refer to it if we communicate with you regarding this application.

LINE-BY-LINE INSTRUCTIONS

Please type or print using black ink. The form is used to produce the certificate.

SPACE 1: Title

Title of This Work: Every work submitted for copyright registration must be given a title to identify that particular work. If the copies or phonorecords of the work bear a title (or an identifying phrase that could serve as a title), transcribe that wording *completely* and *exactly* on the application. Indexing of the registration and future identification of the work will depend on the information you give here. If the work you are registering is an entire "collective work" (such as a collection of plays or songs), give the overall title of the collection. If you arc registering one or more individual contributions to a collective work, give the title of each contribution, followed by the title of the collection. For an unpublished collection, you may give the titles of the individual works after the collection title.

Previous or Alternative Titles: Complete this space if there are any additional titles for the work under which someone searching for the registration might be likely to look, or under which a document pertaining to the work might be recorded.

Nature of This Work: Briefly describe the general nature or character of the work being registered for copyright. Examples: "Music"; "Song Lyrics"; "Words and Music"; "Drama"; "Musical Play"; "Choreography"; "Pantomime"; "Motion Picture"; "Audiovisual Work."

SPACE 2: Author(s)

General Instructions: After reading these instructions, decide who are the "authors" of this work for copyright purposes. Then, unless the work is a "collective work," give the requested information about every "author" who contributed any appreciable amount of copyrightable matter to this version of the work. If you need further space, request additional Continuation Sheets. In the case of a collective work such as a songbook or a collection of plays, give information about the author of the collective work as a whole.

Name of Author: The fullest form of the author's name should be given. Unless the work was "made for hire," the individual who actually created the work is its "author." In the case of a work made for hire, the statute provides that "the employer or other person for whom the work was prepared is considered the author."

What Is a "Work Made for Hire"? A "work made for hire" is defined as: (1) "a work prepared by an employee within the scope of his or her employment"; or (2) "a work specially ordered or commissioned for use as a contribution to a collective work, as a part of a motion picture or other audiovisual work, as a translation, as a supplementary work, as a compilation, as an instructional text, as a test, as answer material for a test, or as an atlas, if the parties expressly agree in a written instrument signed by them that the work shall be considered a work made for hire." If you have checked "Yes" to indicate that the work was "made for hire," you must give the full legal name of the employer (or other person for whom the work was prepared). You may also include the name of the employee along with the name of the employer (for example: "Elstcr Music Co., employer for hire of John Ferguson").

"Anonymous" or "Pseudonymous" Work: An author's contribution to a work is "anonymous" if that author is not identified on the copies or phonorecords of the work. An author's contribution to a work is "pseudonymous" if that author is identified on the copies or phonorecords under a fictitious name. If the work is "anonymous" you may: (1) leave the line blank; or (2) state "anonymous" on the line; or (3) reveal the author's identity. If the work is "pseudonymous" you may: (1) leave the line blank; or (2) give the pseudonym and identify it as such (example: "Huntley Haverstock, pseudonym"); or (3) reveal the author's name, making clear which is the real name and which is the pseudonym (for example: "Judith Barton, whose pseudonym is Madeline Elster"). However, the citizenship or domicile of the author *must* be given in all cases.

Dates of Birth and Death: If the author is dead, the statute requires that the year of death be included in the application unless the work is anonymous or pseudonymous. The author's birth date is optional, but is useful as a form of identification. Leave this space blank if the author's contribution was a "work made for hire."

Author's Nationality or Domicile: Give the country of which the author is a citizen, or the country in which the author is domiciled. Nationality or domicile *must* be given in all cases.

Nature of Authorship: Give a brief general statement of the nature of this particular author's contribution to the work. Examples: "Words"; "Coauthor of Music"; "Words and Music"; "Arrangement"; "Coauthor of Book and Lyrics"; "Dramatization"; "Screen Play"; "Compilation and English Translation"; "Editorial Revisions."

SPACE 3: Creation and Publication

General Instructions: Do not confuse "creation" with "publication." Every application for copyright registration must state "the year in which creation of the work was completed." Give the date and nation of first publication only if the work has been published.

Creation: Under the statute, a work is "created" when it is fixed in a copy or phonorecord for the first time. Where a work has been prepared over a period of time, the part of the work existing in fixed form on a particular date constitutes the created work on that date. The date you give here should be the year in which the author completed the particular version for which registration is now being sought, even if other versions exist or if further changes or additions are planned.

Publication: The statute defines "publication" as "the distribution of copies or phonorecords of a work to the public by sale or other transfer of ownership, or by rental, lease, or lending"; a work is also "published" if there has been an "offering to distribute copies or phonorecords to a group of persons for purposes of further distribution, public performance, or public display." Give the full date (month, day, year) when, and the country where, publication first occurred. If first publication took place simultaneously in the United States and other countries, it is sufficient to state "U.S.A."

SPACE 4: Claimant(s)

Name(s) and Address(es) of Copyright Claimant(s): Give the name(s) and address(es) of the copyright claimants) in this work even if the claimant is the same as the author. Copyright in a work belongs initially to the author of the work (including, in the case of a work made for hire, the employer or other person for whom the work was prepared). The copyright claimant is either the author of the work or a person or organization to whom the copyright initially belonging to the author has been transferred.

Transfer: The statute provides that, if the copyright claimant is not the author, the application for registration must contain "a brief statement of how the claimant obtained ownership of the copyright." If any copyright claimant named in space 4 is not an author named in space 2, give a brief statement explaining how the claimant(s) obtained ownership of the copyright. Examples: "By written contract"; "Transfer of all rights by author"; "Assignment"; "By will." Do not attach transfer documents or other attachments or riders.

SPACE 5: Previous Registration

General Instructions: The questions in space 5 are intended to show whether an earlier registration has been made for this work and, if so, whether there is any basis for a new registration. As a general rule, only one basic copyright registration can be made for the same version of a particular work.

Same Version: If this version is substantially the same as the work covered by a previous registration, a second registration is not generally possible unless: (1) the work has been registered in unpublished form and a second registration is now being sought to cover this first published edition; or (2) someone other than the author is identified as copyright claimant in the earlier registration, and the author is now seeking registration in his or her own name. If either of these two exceptions applies, check the appropriate box and give the earlier registration number and date. Otherwise, do not submit Form PA; instead, write the Copyright Office for information about supplementary registration or recordation of transfers of copyright ownership.

Changed Version: If the work has been changed and you are now seeking registration to cover the additions or revisions, check the last box in space 5, give the earlier registration number and date, and complete both parts of space 6 in accordance with the instructions below.

Previous Registration Number and Date: If more than one previous registration has been made for the work, give the number and date of the latest registration.

SPACE 6: Derivative Work or Compilation

General Instructions: Complete space 6 if this work is a "changed version," "compilation," or "derivative work," and if it incorporates one or more earlier works that have already been published or registered for copyright or that have fallen into the public domain. A "compilation" is defined as "a work formed by the collection and assembling of preexisting materials or of data that are selected, coordinated, or arranged in such a way that the resulting work as a whole constitutes an original work of authorship." A "derivative work" is "a work based on one or more preexisting works." Examples of derivative works include musical arrangements, dramatizations, translations, abridgments, condensations, motion picture versions, or "any other form in which a work may be recast, transformed, or adapted." Derivative works also include works "consisting of editorial revisions, annotations, or other modifications" if these changes, as a whole, represent an original work of authorship.

Preexisting Material (space 6a): Complete this space *and* space 6b for derivative works. In this space identify the preexisting work that has been recast, transformed, or adapted. For example, the preexisting material might be: "French version of Hugo's 'Le Roi s'amuse'." Do not complete this space for compilations. **Material Added to This Work** (space 6b): Give a brief, general statement of the *additional* new material covered by the copyright claim for which registration is sought. In the case of a derivative work, identify this new material. Examples: "Arrangement for piano and orchestra"; "Dramatization for television"; "New film version"; "Revisions throughout; Act III completely new." If the work is a compilation, give a brief, general statement describing both the material that has been compiled *and* the compilation itself. Example: "Compilation of 19th Century Military Songs."

7, 8, 9: SPACE 7, 8, 9: Fee, Correspondence, Certification, Return Address

Deposit Account: If you maintain a Deposit Account in the Copyright Office, identify it in space 7a. Otherwise, leave the space blank and send the fee with your application and deposit

Correspondence (space 7b): Give the name, address, area code, telephone number, fax number, and email address (if available) of the person to be consulted if correspondence about this application becomes necessary.

Certification (space 8): The application cannot be accepted unless it bears the date and the **handwritten signature** of the author or other copyright claimant, or of the owner of exclusive right(s), or of the duly authorized agent of the author, claimant, or owner of exclusive right(s).

Address for Return of Certificate (space 9): The address box must be completed legibly since the certificate will be returned in a window envelope.

MORE INFORMATION

How to Register a Recorded Work: If the musical or dramatic work that you are registering has been recorded (as a tape, disk, or cassette), you may choose either copyright application Form PA (Performing Arts) or Form SR (Sound Recordings), depending on the purpose of the registration.

Use Form PA to register the underlying musical composition or dramatic work. Form SR has been developed specifically to register a "sound recording" as defined by the Copyright Act—a work resulting from the "fixation of a series of sounds," separate and distinct from the underlying musical or dramatic work. Form SR should be used when the copyright claim is limited to the sound recording itself. (In one instance, Form SR may also be used to file for a copyright registration for both kinds of works—see (4) below.) Therefore:

(1) File Form PA if you arc seeking to register the musical or dramatic work, not the "sound recording," even though what you deposit for copyright purposes may be in the form of a phonorecord.

(2) File Form PA if you are seeking to register the audio portion of an audiovisual work, such as a motion picture soundtrack; these are considered integral parts of the audiovisual work.

(3) File Form SR if you are seeking to register the "sound recording" itself, that is, the work that results from the fixation of a series of musical, spoken, or other sounds, but not the underlying musical or dramatic work.

(4) File Form SR if you are the copyright claimant for both the underlying musical or dramatic work and the sound recording, *and* you prefer to register both on the same form.

(5) File both forms PA and SR if the copyright claimant for the underlying work and sound recording differ, or you prefer to have separate registration for them.

"Copies" and "Phonorecords": To register for copyright, you are required to deposit "copies" or "phonorecords." These are defined as follows:

Musical compositions may be embodied (fixed) in "copies," objects from which a work can be read or visually perceived, directly or with the aid of a machine or device, such as manuscripts, books, sheet music, film, and videotape. They may also be fixed in "phonorecords," objects embodying fixations of sounds, such as tapes and phonograph disks, commonly known as phonograph records. For example, a song (the work to be registered) can be reproduced in sheet music ("copies") or phonograph records ("phonorecords"), or both.

Copyright Office fees are subject to change For current fees check the copyright Office website at *www.copyright.gov*, write the copyright Office, or call (202) 707-3000.

Form PA
For a Work of Performing Arts
UNITED STATES COPYRIGHT OFFICE

REGISTRATION NUMBER

_____ PA _____ PAU

EFFECTIVE DATE OF REGISTRATION

_____   _____   _____
Month   Day   Year

DO NOT WRITE ABOVE THIS LINE. IF YOU NEED MORE SPACE, USE A SEPARATE CONTINUATION SHEET.

1

TITLE OF THIS WORK ▼

PREVIOUS OR ALTERNATIVE TITLES ▼

NATURE OF THIS WORK ▼ See instructions

2

a
NAME OF AUTHOR ▼

DATES OF BIRTH AND DEATH
Year Born ▼   Year Died ▼

Was this contribution to the work a "work made for hire"?
☐ Yes
☐ No

AUTHOR'S NATIONALITY OR DOMICILE
Name of Country
OR { Citizen of _____
        Domiciled in _____

WAS THIS AUTHOR'S CONTRIBUTION TO THE WORK
Anonymous?   ☐ Yes   ☐ No
Pseudonymous?   ☐ Yes   ☐ No

If the answer to either of these questions is "Yes," sea detailed Instructions.

NATURE OF AUTHORSHIP Briefly describe nature of material created by this author in which copyright is claimed. ▼

NOTE
Under the law, the "author" of a "work made for hire" is generally the employer, not the employee (see instructions). For any part of this work that was "made for hire" check "Yes" in the space provided, give the employer (or other person for whom the work was prepared) as "Author" of that part, and leave the space for dates of birth and death blank.

b
NAME OF AUTHOR ▼

DATES OF BIRTH AND DEATH
Year Born ▼   Year Died ▼

Was this contribution to the work a "work made for hire"?
☐ Yes
☐ No

AUTHOR'S NATIONALITY OR DOMICILE
Name of Country
OR { Citizen of _____
        Domiciled in _____

WAS THIS AUTHOR'S CONTRIBUTION TO THE WORK
Anonymous?   ☐ Yes   ☐ No
Pseudonymous?   ☐ Yes   ☐ No

If the answer to either of these questions is "Yes," sea detailed Instructions.

NATURE OF AUTHORSHIP Briefly describe nature of material created by this author in which copyright is claimed. ▼

c
NAME OF AUTHOR ▼

DATES OF BIRTH AND DEATH
Year Born ▼   Year Died ▼

Was this contribution to the work a "work made for hire"?
☐ Yes
☐ No

AUTHOR'S NATIONALITY OR DOMICILE
Name of Country
OR { Citizen of _____
        Domiciled in _____

WAS THIS AUTHOR'S CONTRIBUTION TO THE WORK
Anonymous?   ☐ Yes   ☐ No
Pseudonymous?   ☐ Yes   ☐ No

If the answer to either of these questions is "Yes," sea detailed Instructions.

NATURE OF AUTHORSHIP Briefly describe nature of material created by this author in which copyright is claimed. ▼

3

a **YEAR IN WHICH CREATION OF THIS WORK WAS COMPLETED**
_____ Year
This Information must be given In all cases.

b **DATE AND NATION OF FIRST PUBLICATION OF THIS PARTICULAR WORK**
Complete this information ONLY if this work has been published.
Month _____ Day _____ Year _____
_____ Nation

4

COPYRIGHT CLAIMANT(S) Name and address must be given even if the claimant is the same as the author given in space 2. ▼

See instructions before completing this space.

TRANSFER If the claimant(s) named here in space 4 is (are) different from the author(s) named in space 2, give a brief statement of how the claimant(s) obtained ownership of the copyright. ▼

APPLICATION RECEIVED
ONE DEPOSIT RECEIVED
TWO DEPOSITS RECEIVED
FUNDS RECEIVED

DO NOT WRITE HERE
OFFICE USE ONLY

MORE ON BACK ▶
• Complete all applicable spaces (numbers 5-9) on the reverse side of this page.
• See detailed instructions.   • Sign the form at line 8.

DO NOT WRITE HERE

	FORM PA
EXAMINED BY	
CHECKED BY	
CORRESPONDENCE ☐ Yes	FOR COPYRIGHT OFFICE USE ONLY

DO NOT WRITE ABOVE THIS LINE. IF YOU NEED MORE SPACE, USE A SEPARATE CONTINUATION SHEET.

PREVIOUS REGISTRATION Has registration for this work, or for an earlier version of this work, already been made in the Copyright Office?
☐ Yes ☐ No   If your answer is "Yes," why is another registration being sought? (Check appropriate box.) ▼ If your answer is No, do not check box A, B, or C.
a. ☐ This is the first published edition of a work previously registered in unpublished form.
b. ☐ This is the first application submitted by this author as copyright claimant.
c. ☐ This is a changed version of the work, as shown by space 6 on this application.
If your answer is "Yes," give: Previous Registration Number ▼   Year of Registration ▼

5

DERIVATIVE WORK OR COMPILATION Complete both space 6a and 6b for a derivative work; complete only 6b for a compilation.
Preexisting Material Identify any preexisting work or works that this work is based on or incorporates. ▼

a

Material Added to This Work Give a brief, general statement of the material that has been added to this work and in which copyright is claimed. ▼

b

6

See instructions before completing this space.

DEPOSIT ACCOUNT If the registration fee is to be charged to a Deposit Account established in the Copyright Office, give name and number of Account.
Name ▼   Account Number ▼

a

CORRESPONDENCE Give name and address to which correspondence about this application should be sent. Name/Address/Apt/City/State/Zip ▼

b

7

Area code and daytime telephone number   (   )   Fax number   (   )
Email

CERTIFICATION* I, the undersigned, hereby certify that I am the
                                                          ☐ author
                              Check only one { ☐ other copyright claimant
                                                          ☐ owner of exclusive right(s)
                                                          ☐ authorized agent of _____
                                                                          Name of author or other copyright claimant, or owner of exclusive right(s) ▲
of the work identified in this application and that the statements made by me in this application are correct to the best of my knowledge.

8

Typed or printed name and date ▼ If this application gives a date of publication in space 3, do not sign and submit it before that date.

_____ Date _____

Hand written signature (X) ▼

X _____

Certificate will be mailed in window envelope to this address:	Name ▼
	Number/Street/Apt ▼
	City/State/Zip ▼

YOU MUST:
• Complete all necessary spaces
• Sign your application in space 8
SEND ALL 3 ELEMENTS IN THE SAME PACKAGE
1. Application form
2. Nonrefundable filling fee in chuck or money order payable to *Register of Copyrights*
3. Deposit material
MAIL TO:
Library of Congress
Copyright Office
101 Independence Avenue SE
Washington. DC 20559-6000

9

*17 USC §506(8): Any person who knowingly makes a false representation of a material fact in the application for copyright registration provided for by section 409, or in any written statement filed in connection with the application, shall be fined not more than $2,500.
Form PA – Full Rev:07/2006 Print 07/2006 – xx,000 Printed on recycled paper   U.S. Government Printing Office: 2006-xxx-xxx/60,xxx

COPYRIGHTS

Form SR

Detach and read these instructions before completing this form.
Make sure all applicable spaces have been filled in before you return this form.

BASIC INFORMATION

When to Use This Form: Use Form SR for registration of published or unpublished sound recordings. Form SR should be used when the copyright claim is limited to the sound recording itself, and it may also be used where the same copyright claimant is seeking simultaneous registration of the underlying musical, dramatic, or literary work embodied in the phonorecord. With one exception, "sound recordings" are works that result from the fixation of a series of musical, spoken, or other sounds. The exception is for the audio portions of audiovisual works, such as a motion picture soundtrack or an audio cassette accompanying a filmstrip. These are considered a part of the audiovisual work as a whole.

Deposit to Accompany Application: An application for copyright registration must be accompanied by a deposit consisting of phonorecords representing the entire work for which registration is to be made.

   Unpublished Work: Deposit one complete phonorecord.

   Published Work: Deposit two complete phonorecords of the best edition, together with "any printed or other visually perceptible material" published with the phonorecords.

   Work First Published Outside the United States: Deposit one complete phonorecord of the first foreign edition.

   Contribution to a Collective Work: Deposit one complete phonorecord of the best edition of the collective work.

The Copyright Notice: Before March 1, 1989, the use of copyright notice was mandatory on all published works, and any work first published before that date should have carried a notice. For works first published on and after March 1, 1989, use of the copyright notice is optional. For more information about copyright notice, see Circular 3,

Copyright Notices.

For Further Information: To speak to a Copyright Office staff member, call (202) 707-3000 or 1-877-476-0778. Recorded information is available 24 hours a day. Order forms and other publications from Library of Congress, Copyright Office-COPUBS, 101 Independence Avenue SE, Washington, DC 20559 or call the Forms and Publications Hotline at (202) 707-9100. Access and download circulars and other information from the Copyright Office website at *www.copyright.gov*

PRIVACY ACT ADVISORY STATEMENT Required by the Privacy Act of 1974 (P.L. 93-579)

   The authority (or requesting this information is title 17 U.S.C. §409 and §410. Furnishing the requested information is voluntary But if the information is not furnished. It may be necessary to delay or refuse registration and you may not be entitled to certain relief, remedies, and benefits provided in chapters 4 and 5 of title 17 U.S.C.

   The principal uses of the requested information are the establishment and maintenance of a public record and the examination of the application for compliance with the registration requirements of the copyright cods.

   Other routine uses include public inspection and copying, preparation of public indexes, preparation of public catalogs of copyright registrations, and preparation of search reports upon request.

   NOTE: No other advisory statement will be given in connection with this application. Please keep this statement and refer to it if we communicate with you regarding this application.

LINE-BY-LINE INSTRUCTIONS

Please type or print using black ink. The form is used to produce the certificate.

1 SPACE 1: Title

Title of This Work: Every work submitted for copyright registration must be given a title to identify that particular work. If the phonorecords or any accompanying printed material bears a title (or an identifying phrase that could serve as a title), transcribe that wording completely and exactly on the application. indexing of the registration and future identification of the work may depend on the information you give here.

Previous, Alternative, or Contents Titles: Complete this space if mere are any previous or alternative titles for the work under which someone searching for the registration might be likely to look, or under which a document pertaining to the work might be recorded. You may also give the individual contents titles, if any, in this space or you may use a Continuation Sheet (Form CON). Circle the term that describes the titles given.

2 SPACE 2: Author(s)

General Instructions: After reading these instructions, decide who are the "authors" of this work for copyright purposes. Then, unless the work is a "collective work," give the requested information about every "author" who contributed any appreciable amount of copyrightable matter to this version of the work. If you need farmer space, use additional Continuation Sheets. In the case of a collective work such as a collection of previously published or registered sound recordings, give information about the author of the collective work as a whole. If you are submitting this Form SR to cover the recorded musical, dramatic, or literary work as well as the sound recording itself, it is important for space 2 to include full information about the various authors of ail of the material covered by the copyright claim, making clear the nature of each autbor's contribution.

Name of Author: The fullest form of the author's name should be given. Unless the work was "made for hire," the individual who actually created the work is its "author." In the case of a work made for hire, the statute provides that "the employer or other person for whom the work was prepared is considered the author."

What Is a "Work Made for Hire"? A "work made for hire" is defined as: (1) "a work prepared by an employee within the scope of his or her employment"; or (2) "a work specially ordered or commissioned for use as a contribution to a collective work, as a part of a motion picture or other audiovisual work, as a translation, as a supplementary work, as a compilation, as an instructional text, as a test, as answer material for a test, or as an atlas, if me parties expressly agree in a written instrument signed by them that the work shall be considered a work made for hire." If you have checked "Yes" to indicate mat the work was "made for hire," you must give the full legal name of the employer (or other person for whom the work was prepared). You may also include the name of the employee along with the name of the employer (for example: "Elster Record Co., employer for hire of John Ferguson").

"Anonymous" or "Pseudonymous" Work: An author's contribution to a work is "anonymous" if that author is not identified on the copies or phonorecords of the work. An author's contribution to a work is "pseudonymous" if that author is identified on the copies or phonorecords under a fictitious name. If the work is "anonymous" you may: (1) leave the line blank; or (2) state "anonymous" on the line; or (3) reveal the author's identity. If the work is "pseudonymous" you may: (1) leave the line blank; or (2) give the pseudonym and identify it as such (for example: "Huntley Haverstock, pseudonym"); or (3) reveal the author's name, making clear which is the real name and which is the pseudonym (for example: "Judith Barton, whose pseudonym is Madeline Elster"). However, the citizenship or domicile of the author *must* be given in all cases.

Dates of Birth and Death: If the author is dead, the statute requires that the year of death be included in the application unless the work is anonymous or pseudonymous. The author's birth date is optional, but is useful as a form of identification. Leave this space blank if the author's contribution was a "work made for hire."

Author's Nationality or Domicile: Give the country in which the author is a citizen, or the country in which the author is domiciled. Nationality or domicile *must* be given in all cases.

Nature of Authorship: Sound recording authorship is the performance, sound production, or both, that is fixed in the recording deposited for registration. Describe this authorship in space 2 as "sound recording." If the claim also covers the underlying work(s), include the appropriate authorship terms for each author, for example, "words," "music," "arrangement of music," or "text."

Generally, for the claim to cover both the sound recording and the underlying work(s), every author should have contributed to both the sound recording *and* the underlying work(s). If the claim includes artwork or photographs, include the appropriate term in the statement of authorship.

SPACE 3: Creation and Publication

General Instructions: Do not confuse "creation" with "publication." Every application for copyright registration must state "the year in which creation of the work was completed." Give the date and nation of first publication only if the work has been published.

Creation: Under the statute, a work is "created" when it is fixed in a copy or phonorecord for the first time. If a work has been prepared over a period of time, the part of the work existing in fixed form on a particular date constitutes the created work on that date. The date you give here should be the year in which the author completed the particular version for which registration is now being sought, even if other versions exist or if further changes or additions are planned.

Publication: The statute defines "publication" as "the distribution of copies or phonorecords of a work to the public by sale or other transfer of ownership, or by rental, lease, or lending"; a work is also "published" if there has been an "offering to distribute copies or phonorecords to a group of persons for purposes of further distribution, public performance, or public display." Give the full date (month, date, year) when, and the country where, publication first occurred. If first publication look place simultaneously in the United States and other countries, it is sufficient to state "U.S.A."

SPACE 4: Claimant(s)

Name(s) and Address(es) of Copyright Claimant(s): Give the name(s) and address(es) of the copyright claimant(s) in the work even if the claimant is the same as the author. Copyright in a work belongs initially to the author of the work (including, in the case of a work made for hire, the employer or other person for whom the work was prepared). The copyright claimant is either the author of the work or a person or organization to whom the copyright initially belonging to the author has been transferred.

Transfer: The statute provides that, if the copyright claimant is not the author, the application for registration must contain "a brief statement of how the claimant obtained ownership of the copyright." If any copyright claimant named in space 4a is not an author named in space 2, give a brief statement explaining how the daimant(s) obtained ownership of the copyright. Examples: "By written contract'; "Transfer of all rights by author"; "Assignment"; "By will." Do not attach transfer documents or other attachments or riders.

SPACE 5: Previous Registration

General Instructions: The questions in space 5 are intended to show whether an earlier registration has been made for this work and, if so, whether there is any basis for a new registration. As a rule, only one basic copyright registration can be made for the same version of a particular work.

Same Version: If this version is substantially the same as the work covered by a previous registration, a second registration is not generally possible unless: (1) the work has been registered in unpublished form and a second registration is now being sought to cover this first published edition; or (2) someone other than the author is identified as copyright claimant in the earlier registration and the author is now seeking registration in his or her own name. If either of these two exceptions applies, check the appropriate box and give the earlier registration number and date. Otherwise, do not submit Form SR. Instead, write the Copyright Office for information about supplementary registration or recordation of transfers of copyright ownership.

Changed Version: If the work has been changed and you are now seeking registration to cover the additions or revisions, check the last box in space 5, give the earlier registration number and date, and complete both parts of space 6 in accordance with the instructions below.

Previous Registration Number and Date: If more than one previous registration has been made for the work, give the number and date of the latest registration.

SPACE 6: Derivative Work or Compilation

General Instructions: Complete space 6 if this work is a "changed version," "compilation," or "derivative work," and if it incorporates one or more earlier works that have already been published or registered for copyright, or that have fallen into the public domain, or sound recordings that were fixed before February 15, 1972. A "compilation" is defined as "a work formed by the collection and assembling of preexisting materials or of data that are selected, coordinated, or arranged in such a way that the resulting work as a whole constitutes an original work of authorship." A"derivative work" is "a work based on one or more preexisting works." Examples of derivative works include recordings reissued with substantial editorial revisions or abridgments of the recorded sounds, and recordings republished with new recorded material, or "any other form in which a work may be recast, transformed, or adapted." Derivative works also include works "consisting of editorial revisions, annotations, or other modifications" if these changes, as a whole, represent an original work of authorship.

Preexisting Material (space 6a): Complete this space and space 6b for derivative works. In this space identify the preexisting work that has been recast, transformed, or adapted. The preexisting work may be material that has been previously published, previously registered, or that is in the public domain. For example, the preexisting material might be: "1970 recording by Sperryville Symphony of Bach Double Concerto."

Material Added to This Work (space 6b): Give a brief, general statement of the additional new material covered by the copyright claim for which registration is sought. In the case of a derivative work, identify this new material. Examples: "Recorded performances on bands 1 and 3"; "Remixed sounds from original multi-track sound sources"; "New words, arrangement, and additional sounds." If the work is a compilation, give a brief, general statement describing both the material that has been compiled *and* the compilation itself. Example: "Compilation of 1938 recordings by various swing bands."

7, 8, 9 SPACE 7, 8, 9: Fee, Correspondence, Certification, Return Address

Deposit Account: If you maintain a deposit account in the Copyright Office, identify it in space 7a. Otherwise, leave the space blank and send the filing fee with your application and deposit. (See space 8 on form.) Note: Copyright Office fees are subject to change. For current fees, check the Copyright Office website at *www.copyright.gov,* write the Copyright Office, or call (202) 707-3000.

Correspondence (space 7b): Give the name, address, area code, telephone number, fax number, and email address (if available) of the person to be consulted if correspondence about this application becomes necessary.

Certification (space 8): This application cannot be accepted unless it bears the date and the *handwritten signature* of the author or other copyright claimant, or of the owner of exclusive right(s), or of the duly authorized agent of the author, claimant, or owner of exclusive right(s).

Address for Return of Certificate (space 9): The address box must be completed legibly since the certificate will be returned in a window envelope.

MORE INFORMATION

"Works": "Works" are the basic subject matter of copyright; they are what authors create and copyright protects. The statute draws a sharp distinction between the "work" and "any material object in which the work is embodied."

"Copies" and "Phonorecords": These are the two types of material objects in which "works" are embodied. In general, "copies" are objects from which a work can be read or visually perceived, directly or with the aid of a machine or device, such as manuscripts, books, sheet music, film, and videotape. "Phonorecords" are objects embodying fixations of sounds, such as audio tapes and phonograph disks. For example, a song (the "work") can be reproduced in sheet music ("copies") or phonograph disks ("phonorecords"), or both.

"Sound Recordings": These are "works," not "copies" or "phonorecords." "Sound recordings" are "works that result from the fixation of a series of musical, spoken, or other sounds, but not including the sounds accompanying a motion picture or other audiovisual work."

Example: When a record company issues a new release, the release will typically involve two distinct "works": the "musical work" that has been recorded, and the "sound recording" as a separate work in itself.

The material objects that the record company sends out are "phonorecords": physical reproductions of both the "musical work" and the "sound recording."

Should You File More Than One Application? If your work consists of a recorded musical, dramatic, or literary work and if both that "work" and the sound recording as a separate "work" are eligible for registration, the application form you should file depends on the following:

File Only Form SR if: The copyright claimant is the same for both the musical, dramatic, or literary work and for the sound recording, and you are seeking a single registration to cover both of these "works."

File Only Form PA (or Form TX) if: You are seeking to register only the musical, dramatic, or literary work, not the sound recording. Form PA is appropriate for works of the performing arts; Form TX is for nondramatic literary works.

Separate Applications Should Be Filed on Form PA (or Form TX) and on Form SR if: (1) The copyright claimant for the musical, dramatic, or literary work is different from the copyright claimant for the sound recording; or (2) you prefer to have separate registrations for the musical, dramatic, or literary work and for the sound recording.

Copyright Office fees are subject to change For current fees check the copyright Office website at *www.copyright.gov*, write the copyright Office, or call (202) 707-3000.

Privacy Act Notice: Sections 408-410 of title 17 of the *United States Code* authorize the Copyright Office to collect the personally identifying information requested on this form in order to process the application for copyright registration. By providing this information you are agreeing to routine uses of the information that include publication to give legal notice of your copyright claim as required by 17 U.S.C. §705. It will appear in the Office's online catalog. If you do not provide the Information requested, registration may be refused or delayed, and you may not be entitled to certain relief, remedies, and benefits under the copyright law.

Form SR
For a Work of Performing Arts
UNITED STATES COPYRIGHT OFFICE

REGISTRATION NUMBER

_____ SR _____ SRU

EFFECTIVE DATE OF REGISTRATION

_____ _____ _____
Month   Day   Year

DO NOT WRITE ABOVE THIS LINE. IF YOU NEED MORE SPACE, USE A SEPARATE CONTINUATION SHEET.

1
TITLE OF THIS WORK ▼

PREVIOUS, ALTERNATIVE, OR CONTENTS TITLES (CIRCLE ONE) ▼

2

a
NAME OF AUTHOR ▼

DATES OF BIRTH AND DEATH
Year Born ▼   Year Died ▼

Was this contribution to the work a "work made for hire"?
☐ Yes
☐ No

AUTHOR'S NATIONALITY OR DOMICILE
Name of Country
OR { Citizen of _____
     Domiciled in _____

WAS THIS AUTHOR'S CONTRIBUTION TO THE WORK
Anonymous?   ☐ Yes   ☐ No
Pseudonymous? ☐ Yes   ☐ No

If the answer to either of these questions is "Yes," sea detailed Instructions.

NOTE
Under the law, the "author" of a "work made for hire" is generally the employer, not the employee (see instructions). For any part of this work that was "made for hire" check "Yes" in the space provided, give the employer (or other person for whom the work was prepared) as "Author" of that part, and leave the space for dates of birth and death blank.

NATURE OF AUTHORSHIP Briefly describe nature of material created by this author in which copyright is claimed. ▼

b
NAME OF AUTHOR ▼

DATES OF BIRTH AND DEATH
Year Born ▼   Year Died ▼

Was this contribution to the work a "work made for hire"?
☐ Yes
☐ No

AUTHOR'S NATIONALITY OR DOMICILE
Name of Country
OR { Citizen of _____
     Domiciled in _____

WAS THIS AUTHOR'S CONTRIBUTION TO THE WORK
Anonymous?   ☐ Yes   ☐ No
Pseudonymous? ☐ Yes   ☐ No

If the answer to either of these questions is "Yes," sea detailed Instructions.

NATURE OF AUTHORSHIP Briefly describe nature of material created by this author in which copyright is claimed. ▼

c
NAME OF AUTHOR ▼

DATES OF BIRTH AND DEATH
Year Born ▼   Year Died ▼

Was this contribution to the work a "work made for hire"?
☐ Yes
☐ No

AUTHOR'S NATIONALITY OR DOMICILE
Name of Country
OR { Citizen of _____
     Domiciled in _____

WAS THIS AUTHOR'S CONTRIBUTION TO THE WORK
Anonymous?   ☐ Yes   ☐ No
Pseudonymous? ☐ Yes   ☐ No

If the answer to either of these questions is "Yes," sea detailed Instructions.

NATURE OF AUTHORSHIP Briefly describe nature of material created by this author in which copyright is claimed. ▼

3

a
YEAR IN WHICH CREATION OF THIS WORK WAS COMPLETED
_____ Year
This Information must be given In all cases.

b
DATE AND NATION OF FIRST PUBLICATION OF THIS PARTICULAR WORK
Complete this information ONLY If this work has been published.
Month ▶ _____ Day ▶ _____ Year ▶ _____
Nation ▶ _____

4
See instructions before completing this space.

COPYRIGHT CLAIMANT(S) Name and address must be given even if the claimant is the same as the author given in space 2. ▼

b
TRANSFER If the claimant(s) named here in space 4 is (are) different from the author(s) named in space 2, give a brief statement of how the claimant(s) obtained ownership of the copyright. ▼

DO NOT WRITE HERE OFFICE USE ONLY
APPLICATION RECEIVED
ONE DEPOSIT RECEIVED
TWO DEPOSITS RECEIVED
FUNDS RECEIVED

MORE ON BACK ▶
• Complete all applicable spaces (numbers 5-9) on the reverse side of this page.
• See detailed instructions.
• Sign the form at line 8.

DO NOT WRITE HERE

COPYRIGHTS

	EXAMINED BY	FORM SR
	CHECKED BY	
	CORRESPONDENCE ☐ Yes	FOR COPYRIGHT OFFICE USE ONLY

DO NOT WRITE ABOVE THIS LINE. IF YOU NEED MORE SPACE, USE A SEPARATE CONTINUATION SHEET.

PREVIOUS REGISTRATION Has registration for this work, or for an earlier version of this work, already been made in the Copyright Office?
☐ Yes ☐ No   If your answer is "Yes," why is another registration being sought? (Check appropriate box.) ▼
a. ☐ This is the first published edition of a work previously registered in unpublished form.
b. ☐ This is the first application submitted by this author as copyright claimant.
c. ☐ This is a changed version of the work, as shown by space 6 on this application.
If your answer is "Yes," give: Previous Registration Number ▼   Year of Registration ▼

5

DERIVATIVE WORK OR COMPILATION
Preexisting Material Identify any preexisting work or works that this work is based on or incorporates. ▼

a

6

See instructions before completing this space.

Material Added to This Work Give a brief, general statement of the material that has been added to this work and in which copyright is claimed. ▼

b

DEPOSIT ACCOUNT If the registration fee is to be charged to a Deposit Account established in the Copyright Office, give name and number of Account.
Name ▼   Account Number ▼

a

7

CORRESPONDENCE Give name and address to which correspondence about this application should be sent. Name/Address/Apt/City/State/Zip ▼

b

Area code and daytime telephone number   (   )   Fax number   (   )
Email

CERTIFICATION* I, the undersigned, hereby certify that I am the
Check only one ▼
☐ author   ☐ owner of exclusive right(s)
☐ other copyright claimant   ☐ authorized agent of

                                      Name of author or other copyright claimant, or owner of exclusive right(s) ▲
       of the work identified in this application and that the statements made by me in this application are correct to the best of my knowledge.

8

Typed or printed name and date ▼ If this application gives a date of publication in space 3, do not sign and submit it before that date.

_____ Date _____

       Hand written signature ▼

              X_____

Certificate will be mailed in window envelope to this address:	Name ▼	**YOU MUST:** • Complete all necessary spaces • Sign your application in space 8 **SEND ALL 3 ELEMENTS IN THE SAME PACKAGE** 1. Application form 2. Nonrefundable filling fee in chuck or money order payable to Register of Copyrights 3. Deposit material **MAIL TO:** Library of Congress Copyright Office 101 Independence Avenue SE Washington. DC 20559
	Number/Street/Apt ▼	
	City/State/Zip ▼	

9

*17 USC §506(8): Any person who knowingly makes a false representation of a material fact in the application for copyright registration provided for by section 409, or in any written statement filed in connection with the application, shall be fined not more than $2,500.
Form SR – Full Rev: 05/2012   Print 05/2012 – 8,000 Printed on recycled paper   U.S. Government Printing Office: 2012-372-842/80,913

Form TX

Detach and read these instructions before completing this form.
Make sure all applicable spaces have been filled in before you return this form.

BASIC INFORMATION

When to Use This Form: Use Form TX for registration of published or unpublished nondramatic literary works, excluding periodicals or serial issues. This class includes a wide variety of works; fiction, nonfiction, poetry, textbooks, reference works, directories, catalogs, advertising copy, compilations of information, and computer programs. For periodicals and serials, use Form SE.

Deposit to Accompany Application: An application for copyright registration must be accompanied by a deposit consisting of copies or phonorecords representing the entire work for which registration is to be made. The following are the general deposit requirements as set forth in the statute:

Unpublished Work: Deposit one complete copy (or phonorecord)

Published Work: Deposit two complete copies (or one phonorecord) of the best edition.

Work First Published Outside the United States: Deposit one complete copy (or phonorecord) of the first foreign edition.

Contribution to a Collective Work: Deposit one complete copy (or phonorecord) of the best edition of the collective work.

The Copyright Notice: Before March 1, 1989, the use of copyright notice was mandatory on all published works, and any work first published before that date should have carried a notice. For works first published on and after March 1, 1989, use of the copyright notice is optional. For more information about copyright notice, see Circular 3, *Copyright Notices,*

For Further Information: To speak to a Copyright Office staff member, call (202) 707-3000 (TTY: (202) 707-6737). Recorded information is available 24 hours a day. Order forms and other publications from the address in space 9 or call the Forms and Publications Hotline at (202) 707-9100. Access and download circulars, forms, and other information from the Copyright Office website at *www.copyright.gov*

> **PRIVACY ACT ADVISORY STATEMENT Required by the Privacy Act of 1974 (P.L 93-579)**
> The authority lor requesting this Information is title 17 *USC*, secs. 409 and 410. Furnishing the requested Information is voluntary. But If the Information is not furnished, it may be necassary to delay or refuse registration and you may not be entitled to certain relief, remedies, and benefits provided in chapters 4 and 5 of title 17 *USC*. The principal uses of the requested information are the establishment and maintenance of *a* public record and the examination of the application for compliance with the registration requirements of the copyright code.
> Other routine uses include public inspection and copying, preparation of public indexes, preparation of public catalogs of copyright registrations, and preparation of search reports upon request.
> **NOTE:** No other advisory statement will be given in connection with this application. Please keep this statement and refer to It II we communicate with you regarding this application.

LINE-BY-LINE INSTRUCTIONS

Please type or print using black ink. The form is used to produce the certificate.

1 SPACE 1: Title

Title of This Work: Every work submitted for copyright registration must be given a title to identify that particular work. If the copies or phonorecords of the work bear a title or an identifying phrase that could serve as a title, transcribe that wording *completely* and *exactly* on the application. Indexing of the registration and future identification of the work will depend on the information you give here.

Previous or Alternative Titles: Complete this space if there are any additional titles for the work under which someone searching for the registration might be likely to look or under which a document pertaining to the work might be recorded.

Publication as a Contribution: If the work being registered is a contribution to a periodical, serial, or collection, give the title of the contribution in the "Title of This Work" space. Then, in the line headed "Publication as a Contribution," give information about the collective work in which the contribution appeared.

2 SPACE 2: Author(s)

General Instructions: After reading these instructions, decide who are the "authors" of this work for copyright purposes. Then, unless the work is a "collective work," give the requested information about every "author" who contributed any appreciable amount of copyrightable matter to this version of the work. If you need further space, request Continuation Sheets. In the case of a collective work, such as an anthology, collection of essays, or encyclopedia, give information about the author of the collective work as a whole.

Name of Author: The fullest form of the author's name should be given. Unless the work was "made for hire," the individual who actually created the work is its "author." In the case of a work made for hire, the statute provides that "the employer or other person for whom the work was prepared is considered the author."

What Is a "Work Made for Hire"? A "work made for hire" is defined as (1) "a work prepared by an employee within the scope of his or her employment"; or (2) "a work specially ordered or commissioned for use as a contribution to a collective work, as a part of a motion picture or other audiovisual work, as a translation, as a supplementary work, as a compilation, as an instructional text, as a test, as answer material for a test, or as an atlas, if the parties expressly agree in a written instrument signed by them that the works shall be considered a work made for hire." If you have checked "Yes" to indicate that the work was "made for hire," you must give the full legal name of the employer (or other person for whom the work was prepared). You may also include the name of the employee along with the name of the employer (for example: "Elster Publishing Co., employer for hire of John Ferguson").

"Anonymous" or "Pseudonymous" Work: An author's contribution to a work is "anonymous" if that author is not identified on the copies or phonorecords of the work. An author's contribution to a work is "pseudonymous" if that author is identified on the copies or phonorecords under a fictitious name. If the work is "anonymous" you may: (1) leave the line blank; or (2) state "anonymous" on the line; or (3) reveal the author's identity. If the work is "pseudonymous" you may: (1) leave the line blank; or (2) give the pseudonym and identify it as such (for example: "Huntley Haverstock, pseudonym"); or (3) reveal the author's name, making clear which is the real name and which is the pseudonym (for example, "Judith Barton, whose pseudonym is Madeline Elster"). However, the citizenship or domicile of the author *must* be given in all cases.

Dates of Birth and Death: If the author is dead, the statute requires that the year of death be included in the application unless the work is anonymous or pseudonymous. The author's birth date is optional but is useful as a form of identification. Leave this space blank if the author's contribution was a "work made for hire."

Author's Nationality or Domicile: Give the country of which the author is a citizen or the country in which the author is domiciled. Nationality or domicile *must* be given in all cases.

Nature of Authorship; After the words "Nature of Authorship," give a brief general statement of the nature of this particular author's contribution to the work. Examples: "Entire text"; "Coauthor of entire text"; "Computer program"; "Editorial revisions"; "Compilation and English translation"; "New text."

SPACE 3: Creation and Publication

General Instructions: Do not confuse "creation" with "publication." Every application for copyright registration must stale "the year in which creation of the work was completed." Give the date and nation of first publication only if the work has been published.

Creation: Under the statute, a work is "created" when it is fixed in a copy or phonorecord for the first time. Where a work has been prepared over a period of time, the part of the work existing in fixed form on a particular date constitutes the created work on that date. The date you give here should be the year in which the author completed the particular version for which registration is now being sought, even if other versions exist or if further changes or additions are planned.

Publication: The statute defines "publication" as "the distribution of copies or phonorecords of a work to the public by sale or other transfer of ownership, or by rental, lease, or lending." A work is also "published" if there has been an "offering to distribute copies or phonorecords to a group of persons for purposes of further distribution, public performance, or public display." Give the full date (month, day, year) when, and the country where, publication first occurred. If first publication took place simultaneously in the United States and other countries, it is sufficient to state "U.S.A."

SPACE 4: Claimant(s)

Name(s) and Address(es) of Copyright Claimant(s): Give the name(s) and address(es) of the copyright claimant(s) in this work even if the claimant is the same as the author. Copyright in a work belongs initially to the author of the work (including, in the case of a work made for hire, the employer or other person for whom the work was prepared). The copyright claimant is either the author of the work or a person or organization to whom the copyright initially belonging to the author has been transferred.

Transfer: The statute provides that, if the copyright claimant is not the author, the application for registration must contain "a brief statement of how the claimant obtained ownership of the copyright." If any copyright claimant named in space 4 is not an author named in space 2, give a brief statement explaining how the claimant(s) obtained ownership of the copyright. Examples: "By written contract"; "Transfer of all rights by author"; "Assignment"; "By will." Do not attach transfer documents or other attachments or riders.

SPACE 5: Previous Registration

General Instructions: The questions in space 5 are intended to show whether an earlier registration has been made for this work and, if so, whether there is any basis for a new registration. As a general rule, only one basic copyright registration can be made for the same version of a particular work.

Same Version: If this version is substantially the same as the work covered by a previous registration, a second registration is not generally possible unless: (1) the work has been registered in unpublished form and a second registration is now being sought to cover this first published edition; or (2) someone other than the author is identified as copyright claimant in the earlier registration, and the author is now seeking registration in his or her own name. If either of these two exceptions applies, check the appropriate box and give the earlier registration number and date. Otherwise, do not submit Form TX. Instead, write the Copyright Office for information about supplementary registration or recordation of transfers of copyright ownership.

Changed Version: If the work has been changed and you are now seeking registration to cover the additions or revisions, check the last box in space 5, give the earlier registration number and date, and complete both parts of space 6 in accordance with the instructions below.

Previous Registration Number and Date: If more than one previous registration has been made for the work, give the number and dale of the latest registration.

SPACE 6: Derivative Work or Compilation

General Instructions: Complete space 6 if this work is a "changed version," "compilation," or "derivative work" and if it incorporates one or more earlier works that have already been published or registered for copyright or that have fallen into the public domain. A "compilation" is defined as "a work formed by the collection and assembling of preexisting materials or of data that are selected, coordinated, or arranged in such a way that the resulting work as a whole constitutes an original work of authorship." A "derivative work" is "a work based on one or more preexisting works." Examples of derivative works include translations, fictionalizations, abridgments, condensations, or "any other form in which a work may be recast, transformed, or adapted." Derivative works also include works "consisting of editorial revisions, annotations, or other modifications" if these changes, as a whole, represent an original work of authorship.

Preexisting Material (space 6a): For derivative works, complete this space *and* space 6b. In space 6a identify the preexisting work that has been recast, transformed, or adapted. The preexisting work may be material that has been previously published, previously registered, or that is in the public domain. An example of preexisting material might be: "Russian version of Goncharoy's 'Oblomov.'"

Material Added to This Work (space 6b): Give a brief, general statement of the new material covered by the copyright claim for which registration is sought. *Derivative work* examples include: "Foreword, editing, critical annotations"; "Translation"; "Chapters 11-17." If the work is a *compilation,* describe both the compilation itself and the material that has been compiled. Example: "Compilation of certain 1917 speeches by Woodrow Wilson." A work may be both a derivative work and compilation, in which case a sample statement might be: "Compilation and additional new material."

7, 8, 9 SPACE 7, 8, 9: Fee, Correspondence, Certification, Return Address

Deposit Account: If you maintain a Deposit Account in the Copyright Office, identify it in space 7a. Otherwise leave the space blank and send the fee with your application and deposit.

Correspondence (space 7b): Give the name, address, area code, telephone number, fax number, and email address (if available) of the person to be consulted if correspondence about this application becomes necessary.

Certification (space 8): The application cannot be accepted unless it bears the date and the *handwritten signature* of the author or other copyright claimant, or of the owner of exclusive right(s), or of the duly authorized agent of author, claimant, or owner of exclusive right(s).

Address for Return of Certificate (space 9): The address box must be completed legibly since the certificate will be returned in a window envelope.

Copyright Office fees are subject to change For current fees check the copyright Office website at *www.copyright.gov,* write the copyright Office, or call (202) 707-3000.

Form TX
For a Work of Performing Arts
UNITED STATES COPYRIGHT OFFICE

REGISTRATION NUMBER

TX   TXU

EFFECTIVE DATE OF REGISTRATION

Month   Day   Year

DO NOT WRITE ABOVE THIS LINE. IF YOU NEED MORE SPACE, USE A SEPARATE CONTINUATION SHEET.

1

TITLE OF THIS WORK ▼

PREVIOUS OR ALTERNATIVE TITLES ▼

PUBLICATION AS A CONTRIBUTION If this work was published as a contribution to a periodical, serial, or collection, give information about this collective work in which the contribution appeared.

If published in a periodical or serial give: Volume ▼   Number ▼   Issue Date ▼   On Pages ▼

2

a

NAME OF AUTHOR ▼

DATES OF BIRTH AND DEATH
Year Born ▼   Year Died ▼

Was this contribution to the work a "work made for hire"?
☐ Yes
☐ No

AUTHOR'S NATIONALITY OR DOMICILE
Name of Country
OR { Citizen of _____
Domiciled in _____

WAS THIS AUTHOR'S CONTRIBUTION TO THE WORK
Anonymous?   ☐ Yes   ☐ No
Pseudonymous? ☐ Yes   ☐ No

If the answer to either of these questions is "Yes," sea detailed Instructions.

NOTE
Under the law, the "author" of a "work made for hire" is generally the employer, not the employee (see instructions). For any part of this work that was "made for hire" check "Yes" in the space provided, give the employer (or other person for whom the work was prepared) as "Author" of that part, and leave the space for dates of birth and death blank.

NATURE OF AUTHORSHIP Briefly describe nature of material created by this author in which copyright is claimed. ▼

b

NAME OF AUTHOR ▼

DATES OF BIRTH AND DEATH
Year Born ▼   Year Died ▼

Was this contribution to the work a "work made for hire"?
☐ Yes
☐ No

AUTHOR'S NATIONALITY OR DOMICILE
Name of Country
OR { Citizen of _____
Domiciled in _____

WAS THIS AUTHOR'S CONTRIBUTION TO THE WORK
Anonymous?   ☐ Yes   ☐ No
Pseudonymous? ☐ Yes   ☐ No

If the answer to either of these questions is "Yes," sea detailed Instructions.

NATURE OF AUTHORSHIP Briefly describe nature of material created by this author in which copyright is claimed. ▼

c

NAME OF AUTHOR ▼

DATES OF BIRTH AND DEATH
Year Born ▼   Year Died ▼

Was this contribution to the work a "work made for hire"?
☐ Yes
☐ No

AUTHOR'S NATIONALITY OR DOMICILE
Name of Country
OR { Citizen of _____
Domiciled in _____

WAS THIS AUTHOR'S CONTRIBUTION TO THE WORK
Anonymous?   ☐ Yes   ☐ No
Pseudonymous? ☐ Yes   ☐ No

If the answer to either of these questions is "Yes," sea detailed Instructions.

NATURE OF AUTHORSHIP Briefly describe nature of material created by this author in which copyright is claimed. ▼

3

a YEAR IN WHICH CREATION OF THIS WORK WAS COMPLETED
_____ ◀ Year
This Information must be given In all cases.

b DATE AND NATION OF FIRST PUBLICATION OF THIS PARTICULAR WORK
Complete this information ONLY If this work has been published.
Month▶ _____ Day▶ _____ Year▶ _____
_____ ◀ Nation

4

COPYRIGHT CLAIMANT(S) Name and address must be given even if the claimant is the same as the author given in space 2.

TRANSFER If the claimant(s) named here in space 4 is (are) different from the author(s) named in space 2, give a brief statement of how the claimant(s) obtained ownership of the copyright. ▼

See instructions before completing this space.

DO NOT WRITE HERE
OFFICE USE ONLY

APPLICATION RECEIVED

ONE DEPOSIT RECEIVED

TWO DEPOSITS RECEIVED

FUNDS RECEIVED

MORE ON BACK ▶
• Complete all applicable spaces (numbers 5-9) on the reverse side of this page.
• See detailed instructions.
• Sign the form at line 8.

DO NOT WRITE HERE

COPYRIGHTS

EXAMINED BY _____	FORM TX
CHECKED BY _____	
CORRESPONDENCE ☐ Yes _____	FOR COPYRIGHT OFFICE USE ONLY

DO NOT WRITE ABOVE THIS LINE. IF YOU NEED MORE SPACE, USE A SEPARATE CONTINUATION SHEET.

5

PREVIOUS REGISTRATION Has registration for this work, or for an earlier version of this work, already been made in the Copyright Office?
☐ Yes ☐ No If your answer is "Yes," why is another registration being sought? (Check appropriate box.) ▼
a. ☐ This is the first published edition of a work previously registered in unpublished form.
b. ☐ This is the first application submitted by this author as copyright claimant.
c. ☐ This is a changed version of the work, as shown by space 6 on this application.
If your answer is "Yes," give: Previous Registration Number ▶ _____ Year of Registration ▶ _____

6

a

DERIVATIVE WORK OR COMPILATION
Preexisting Material Identify any preexisting work or works that this work is based on or incorporates. ▼
_____

b

Material Added to This Work Give a brief, general statement of the material that has been added to this work and in which copyright is claimed. ▼
_____

See instructions before completing this space.

7

a

DEPOSIT ACCOUNT If the registration fee is to be charged to a Deposit Account established in the Copyright Office, give name and number of Account.
Name ▼ _____ Account Number ▼ _____

b

CORRESPONDENCE Give name and address to which correspondence about this application should be sent. Name/Address/Apt/City/State/Zip ▼
_____

Area code and daytime telephone number ▶ _____ Fax number ▶ _____
Email ▶ _____

8

CERTIFICATION* I, the undersigned, hereby certify that I am the
Check only one
☐ author
☐ other copyright claimant
☐ owner of exclusive right(s)
☐ authorized agent of _____
Name of author or other copyright claimant, or owner of exclusive right(s) ▲

of the work identified in this application and that the statements made by me in this application are correct to the best of my knowledge.

Typed or printed name and date ▼ If this application gives a date of publication in space 3, do not sign and submit it before that date.
_____ Date ▶ _____

Hand written signature ▼
X _____

9

Certificate will be mailed in window envelope to this address:	Name ▼
	Number/Street/Apt ▼
	City/State/Zip ▼

YOU MUST:
• Complete all necessary spaces
• Sign your application in space 8
SEND ALL 3 ELEMENTS IN THE SAME PACKAGE
1. Application form
2. Nonrefundable filling fee in chuck or money order payable to *Register of Copyrights*
3. Deposit material
MAIL TO:
Library of Congress
Copyright Office
101 Independence Avenue SE
Washington, DC 20559-5222

*17 USC §506(8): Any person who knowingly makes a false representation of a material fact in the application for copyright registration provided for by section 409, or in any written statement filed in connection with the application, shall be fined not more than $2,500.
Form TX – Full Rev:11/2006 Print 11/2006 – 30,000 Printed on recycled paper   U.S. Government Printing Office: 2006-xxx-xxx/60,xxx

Form VA

Detach and read these instructions before completing this form.
Make sure all applicable spaces have been filled in before you return this form.

BASIC INFORMATION

When to Use This Form: Use Form VA for copyright registration of published or unpublished works of the visual arts. This category consists of "pictorial, graphic, or sculptural works," including two-dimensional and three-dimensional works of fine, graphic, and applied art, photographs, prints and art reproductions, maps, globes, charts, technical drawings, diagrams, and models.

What Does Copyright Protect? Copyright in a work of the visual arts protects those pictorial, graphic, or sculptural elements that, either alone or in combination, represent an "original work of authorship." The statute declares: "In no case does copyright protection for an original work of authorship extend to any idea, procedure, process, system, method of operation, concept, principle, or discovery, regardless of the form in which it is described, explained, illustrated, or embodied in such work."

Works of Artistic Craftsmanship and Designs: You may register "Works of artistic craftsmanship" on Form VA, but the statute makes clear that protection extends to "their form" and not to "their mechanical or utilitarian aspects." The "design of a useful article" is considered copyrightable "only if, and only to the extent that, such design incorporates pictorial, graphic, or sculptural features that can be identified separately from, and are capable of existing independently of, the utilitarian aspects of the article."

Labels and Advertisements: Works prepared for use in connection with the sale or advertisement of goods and services may be registered if they contain "original work of authorship." Use Form VA if the copyrightable material in the work you are registering is mainly pictorial or graphic; use Form TX if it consists mainly of text.
Note: Words and short phrases such as names, titles, and slogans cannot be protected by copyright, and the same is true of standard symbols, emblems, and other commonly used graphic designs that are in the public domain. When used commercially, material of that sort can sometimes be protected under state laws of unfair competition or under the federal trademark laws. For information about trademark registration, call the U.S. Patent and Trademark Office, at 1-800-786-9199 (toll free) or go to *www.uspto.gov.*

Architectural Works: Copyright protection extends to the design of buildings created for the use of human beings. Architectural works created on or after December 1, 1990, or that on December 1, 1990, were unconstructed and embodied only in unpublished plans or drawings are eligible. Request Circular 41, *Copyright Claims in Architectural Works,* for more information. Architectural works and technical drawings cannot be registered on the same application.

Deposit to Accompany Application: An application for copyright registration must be accompanied by a deposit consisting of copies representing the entire work for which registration is to be made.

> **Unpublished Work:** Deposit one complete copy.
>
> **Published Work:** Deposit two complete copies of the best edition.
>
> **Work First Published Outside the United States:** Deposit one complete copy of the first foreign edition.
>
> **Contribution to a Collective Work:** Deposit one complete copy of the best edition of the collective work.

The Copyright Notice: Before March 1, 1989, the use of copyright notice was mandatory on all published works, and any work first published before that date should have carried a notice. For works first published on and after March 1, 1989, use of the copyright notice is optional. For more information about copyright notice, see Circular 3, *Copyright Notice.*

For Further Information: To speak to a Copyright Office staff member, call (202) 707-3000 or 1-877-476-0778. Recorded information is available 24 hours a day. Order forms and other publications from the address in space 9 or call the Forms and Publications Hotline at (202) 707-9100. Access and download circulars, forms, and other information from the Copyright Office website at *www.copyright.gov*

LINE-BY-LINE INSTRUCTIONS

Please type or print using black ink. The form is used to produce the certificate.

1 SPACE 1: Title

Title of This Work: Every work submitted for copyright registration must be given a title to identify that particular work. If the copies of the work bear a title (or an identifying phrase that could serve as a title), transcribe that wording *completely* and *exactly* on the application. Indexing of the registration and future identification of the work will depend on the information you give here. For an architectural work that has been constructed, add the date of construction after the title; if unconstructed at this time, add "not yet constructed."

Publication as a Contribution: If the work being registered is a contribution to a periodical, serial, or collection, give the title of the contribution in the "Title of This Work" space. Then, in the line headed "Publication as a Contribution," give information about the collective work in which the contribution appeared.

Nature of This Work: Briefly describe the general nature or character of the pictorial, graphic, or sculptural work being registered for copyright. Examples: "Oil Painting"; "Charcoal Drawing"; "Etching"; "Sculpture"; "Map"; "Photograph"; "Scale Model"; "Lithographic Print"; "Jewelry Design"; "Fabric Design."

Previous or Alternative Titles: Complete this space if there are any additional titles for the work under which, someone searching for the registration might be likely to look, or under which a document pertaining to the work might be recorded.

2 SPACE 2: Author(s)

General Instruction: After reading these instructions, decide who are the "authors" of this work for copyright purposes. Then, unless the work is a "collective work," give the requested information about every "author" who contributed any appreciable amount of copyrightable matter to this version of the work. If you need further space, request Continuation Sheets (Form CON). In the case of a collective work, such as a catalog of paintings or collection of cartoons by various authors, give information about the author of the collective work as a whole.

Name of Author: The fullest form of the author's, name should be given. Unless the work was "made for hire," the individual who actually created the work is its "author." In the case of a work made for hire, the statute provides that "the employer or other person for whom the work was prepared is considered the author."

What Is a "Work Made for Hire"? A "work made for hire" is defined as: (1) "a work prepared by an employee within the scope of his or her employment"; or (2) "a work specially ordered or commissioned for use as a contribution to a collective work, as a part of a motion picture or other audiovisual work, as a translation, as a supplementary work, as a compilation, as an instructional text, as a test, as answer material for a test, or as an atlas, if the parties expressly agree in a written instrument signed by them that the work shall be considered a work made for hire." If you have checked "Yes" to indicate that the work was "made for hire," you must give the full legal name of the employer (or other person for whom the work was prepared). You may also include the name of the employee along with the name of the employer (for example: "Elster Publishing Co., employer for hire of John Ferguson").

"Anonymous" or "Pseudonymous" Work: An author's contribution to a work is "anonymous" if that author is not identified on the copies or phonorecords of the work. An author's contribution to a work is "pseudonymous" if that author is identified on the copies or phonorecords under a fictitious name. If the work is "anonymous" you may: (1) leave the line blank; or (2) state "anonymous" on the line; or (3) reveal the author's identity. If the work is "pseudonymous" you may: (1) leave the line blank; or (2) give the pseudonym and identify it as such (for example: "Huntley Haverstock, pseudonym"); or (3) reveal the author's name, making clear which is the real name and which is the pseudonym (for example: "Henry Leek, whose pseudonym is Priam Farrel"). However, the citizenship or domicile of the author *must* be given in all cases.

Dates of Birth and Death: If the author is dead, the statute requires that the year of death be included in the application unless the work is anonymous or pseudonymous. The author's birth date is optional but is useful as a form of identification. Leave this space blank if the author's contribution was a "work made for hire."

Author's Nationality or Domicile: Give the country of which the author is a citizen or the country in which the author is domiciled. Nationality or domicile *must* be given in all cases.

Nature of Authorship: Categories of pictorial, graphic, and sculptural authorship are listed below. Check the box(es) that best describc(s) each author's contribution to the work.

3-Dimensional sculptures: Fine art sculptures, toys, dolls, scale models, and sculptural designs applied to useful articles.

2-Dimensional artwork: Watercolor and oil paintings; pen and ink drawings; logo illustrations; greeting cards; collages; stencils; patterns; computer graphics; graphics appearing in screen displays; artwork appearing on posters, calendars, games, commercial prints and labels, and packaging, as well as 2-dimensional artwork applied to useful articles, and designs reproduced on textiles, lace, and other fabrics; on wallpaper, carpeting, floor tile, wrapping paper, and clothing.

Reproductions of works of art: Reproductions of preexisting artwork made by, for example, lithography, photoengraving, or etching.

Maps: Cartographic representations of an area, such as state and county maps, atlases, marine charts, relief maps, and globes.

Photographs: Pictorial photographic prints and slides and holograms.

Jewelry designs: 3-dimensional designs applied to rings, pendants, earrings, necklaces, and the like.

Technical drawings: Diagrams illustrating scientific or technical information in linear form, such as architectural blueprints or mechanical drawings.

Text: Textual material that accompanies pictorial, graphic, or sculptural works, such as comic strips, greeting cards, games rules, commercial prints or labels, and maps.

Architectural works: Designs of buildings, including the overall form as well as the arrangement and composition of spaces and elements of the design.

NOTE: You must apply for registration for the underlying architectural plans on a separate Form VA. Check the box "Technical drawing."

SPACE 3: Creation and Publication

General Instructions: Do not confuse "creation" with "publication." Every application for copyright registration must state "the year in which creation of the work was completed." Give the date and nation of first publication only if the work has been published.

Creation: Under the statute, a work is "created" when it is fixed in a copy or phonorecord for the first time. If a work has been prepared over a period of time, the part of the work existing in fixed form on a particular date constitutes the created work on that date. The date you give here should be the year in which the author completed the particular version for which registration is now being sought, even if other versions exist or if further changes or additions are planned.

Publication: The statute defines "publication" as "the distribution of copies or phonorecords of a work to the public by sale or other transfer of ownership, or by rental, lease, or lending"; a work is also "published" if there has been an "offering to distribute copies or phonorecords to a group of persons for purposes of further distribution, public performance, or public display." Give the full date (month, day, year) when, and the country where, publication First occurred. If first publication took place simultaneously in the United States and other countries, it is sufficient to state "U.S.A."

SPACE 4: Claimant(s)

Name(s) and Address(es) of Copyright Claimant(s): Give the name(s) and address(es) of the copyright claimant(s) in this work even if the claimant is the same as the author. Copyright in a work belongs initially to the author of the work, including, in the case of a work make for hire, the employer or other person for whom the work was prepared. The copyright claimant is either the author of the work or a person or organization to whom the copyright initially belonging to the author has been transferred.

Transfer: The statute provides that, if the copyright claimant is not the author, the application for registration must contain "a brief statement of how the claimant obtained ownership of the copyright." If any copyright claimant named in space 4 is not an author named in space 2, give a brief statement explaining how the claimant(s) obtained ownership of the copyright. Examples: "By written contract"; "Transfer of all rights by author"; "Assignment"; "By will." Do not attach transfer documents or other attachments or riders.

SPACE 5: Previous Registration

General Instructions: The questions in space 5 are intended to find out whether an earlier registration has been made for this work and, if so, whether there is any basis for a new registration. As a rule, only one basic copyright registration can be made for the same version of a particular work.

Same Version: If this version is substantially the same as the work covered by a previous registration, a second registration is not generally possible unless: (1) the work has been registered in unpublished form and a second registration is now being sought to cover this first published edition; or (2) someone other than the author is identified as a copyright claimant in the earlier registration, and the author is now seeking registration in his or her own name. If either of these two exceptions applies, check the appropriate box and give the earlier registration number and date. Otherwise, do not submit Form VA. Instead, write the Copyright Office for information about supplementary registration or recordation of transfers of copyright ownership.

Changed Version: If the work has been changed and you are now seeking registration to cover the additions or revisions, check the last box in space 5, give the earlier registration number and date, and complete both parts of space 6 in accordance with the instruction below.

Previous Registration Number and Date: If more than one previous registration has been made for the work, give the number and date of the latest registration.

6 SPACE 6: Derivative Work or Compilation

General Instructions: Complete space 6 if this work is a "changed version," "compilation," or "derivative work," and if it incorporates one or more earlier works that have already been published or registered for copyright, or that have fallen into the public domain. A "compilation" is defined as "a work formed by the collection and assembling of preexisting materials or of data that are selected, coordinated, or arranged in such a way that the resulting work as a whole constitutes an original work of authorship." A "derivative work" is "a work based on one or more preexisting works." Examples of derivative works include reproductions of works of art, sculptures based on drawings, lithographs based on paintings, maps based on previously published sources, or "any other form in which a work may be recast, transformed, or adapted." Derivative works also include works "consisting of editorial revisions, annotations, or other modifications" if these changes, as a whole, represent an original work of authorship.

Preexisting Material (space 6a): Complete this space and space 6b for derivative works. In this space identify the preexisting work that has been recast, transformed, or adapted. Examples of preexisting material might be "Grunewald Altarpiece" or "19th century quilt design." Do not complete this space for compilations.

Material Added to This Work (space 6b): Give a brief, general statement of the *additional* new material covered by the copyright claim for which registration is sought. In the case of a derivative work, identify this new material. Examples: "Adaptation of design and additional artistic work"; "Reproduction of painting by photolithography"; "Additional cartographic material"; "Compilation of photographs." If the work is a compilation, give a brief, general statement describing both the material that has been compiled *and* the compilation itself. Example: "Compilation of 19th century political cartoons."

7, 8, 9 SPACE 7, 8, 9: Fee, Correspondence, Certification, Return Address

Deposit Account: If you maintain a Deposit Account in the Copyright Office, identify it in space 7a. Otherwise, leave the space blank and send the fee with your application and deposit.

Correspondence (space 7b): Give the name, address, area code, telephone number, email address, and fax number (if available) of the person to be consulted if correspondence about this application becomes necessary.

Certification (space 8): The application cannot be accepted unless it bears the date and the *handwritten signature* of the author or other copyright claimant, or of the owner of exclusive right(s), or of the duly authorized agent of the author, claimant, or owner of exclusive right(s).

Address for Return of Certificate (space 9): The address box must be completed legibly since the certificate will be returned in a window envelope.

PRIVACY ACT ADVISORY STATEMENT Required by the Privacy Act of 1974 (P.L. 93 - 579)

The authority for requesting this information is title 17 U.S.C. §409 and §410. Furnishing the requested information is voluntary. But if the information is not furnished, it may be necessary to delay or refuse registration and you may not be entitled to certain relief, remedies, and benefits provided in chapters 4 and 5 of title 17 U.S.C.

The principal uses of the requested information are the establishment and maintenance of a public record and the examination of the application for compliance with the registration requirements of the copyright code.

Other routine uses include public inspection and copying, preparation of public indexes, preparation of public catalogs of copyright registrations, and preparation of search reports upon request.

NOTE: No other advisory statement will be given in connection with this application. Please keep this statement and refer to it if we communicate with you regarding this application.

Copyright Office fees are subject to change For current fees check the copyright Office website at *www.copyright.gov,* write the copyright Office, or call (202) 707-3000.

Privacy Act Notice: Sections 408-410 of title 17 of the *United States Code* authorize the Copyright Office to collect the personally identifying information requested on this form in order to process the application for copyright registration. By providing this information you are agreeing to routine uses of the information that include publication to give legal notice of your copyright claim as required by 17 U.S.C. §705. It will appear in the Office's online catalog. If you do not provide the Information requested, registration may be refused or delayed, and you may not be entitled to certain relief, remedies, and benefits under the copyright law.

Form VA
For a Work of Performing Arts
UNITED STATES COPYRIGHT OFFICE

REGISTRATION NUMBER

VA   VAU

EFFECTIVE DATE OF REGISTRATION

Month   Day   Year

DO NOT WRITE ABOVE THIS LINE. IF YOU NEED MORE SPACE, USE A SEPARATE CONTINUATION SHEET.

1 TITLE OF THIS WORK ▼

PREVIOUS OR ALTERNATIVE TITLES ▼

PUBLICATION AS A CONTRIBUTION If this work was published as a contribution to a periodical, serial, or collection, give information about this collective work in which the contribution appeared.

If published in a periodical or serial give: Volume ▼   Number ▼   Issue Date ▼   On Pages ▼

---

2 a NAME OF AUTHOR ▼

DATES OF BIRTH AND DEATH
Year Born ▼   Year Died ▼

Was this contribution to the work a "work made for hire"?
☐ Yes
☐ No

AUTHOR'S NATIONALITY OR DOMICILE
Name of Country
OR { Citizen of _____
    { Domiciled in _____

WAS THIS AUTHOR'S CONTRIBUTION TO THE WORK
Anonymous?   ☐ Yes ☐ No
Pseudonymous? ☐ Yes ☐ No

If the answer to either of these questions is "Yes," sea detailed Instructions.

NOTE
Under the law, the "author" of a "work made for hire" is generally the employer, not the employee (see instructions). For any part of this work that was "made for hire" check "Yes" in the space provided, give the employer (or other person tor whom the work was prepared) as "Author" of that part, and leave the space for dates of birth and death blank.

NATURE OF AUTHORSHIP Check appropriate box(es). See instructions
☐ 3-Dimensional sculpture   ☐ Map   ☐ Technical drawing
☐ 2-Dimensional artwork   ☐ Photograph   ☐ Text
☐ Reproduction of work of art ☐ Jewelry design ☐ Architectural work

b NAME OF AUTHOR ▼

DATES OF BIRTH AND DEATH
Year Born ▼   Year Died ▼

Was this contribution to the work a "work made for hire"?
☐ Yes
☐ No

AUTHOR'S NATIONALITY OR DOMICILE
Name of Country
OR { Citizen of _____
    { Domiciled in _____

WAS THIS AUTHOR'S CONTRIBUTION TO THE WORK
Anonymous?   ☐ Yes ☐ No
Pseudonymous? ☐ Yes ☐ No

If the answer to either of these questions is "Yes," sea detailed Instructions.

NATURE OF AUTHORSHIP Check appropriate box(es). See instructions
☐ 3-Dimensional sculpture   ☐ Map   ☐ Technical drawing
☐ 2-Dimensional artwork   ☐ Photograph   ☐ Text
☐ Reproduction of work of art ☐ Jewelry design ☐ Architectural work

---

3 a YEAR IN WHICH CREATION OF THIS WORK WAS COMPLETED   This Information must be given In all cases.
_____ Year

b DATE AND NATION OF FIRST PUBLICATION OF THIS PARTICULAR WORK
Complete this information ONLY If this work has been published.
Month ▶ _____ Day ▶ _____ Year ▶ _____
_____ Nation

---

4 COPYRIGHT CLAIMANT(S) Name and address must be given even if the claimant is the same as the author given in space 2.

See instructions before completing this space.

TRANSFER If the claimant(s) named here in space 4 is (are) different from the author(s) named in space 2, give a brief statement of how the claimant(s) obtained ownership of the copyright. ▼

DO NOT WRITE HERE
OFFICE USE ONLY

APPLICATION RECEIVED
_____
ONE DEPOSIT RECEIVED
_____
TWO DEPOSITS RECEIVED
_____
FUNDS RECEIVED
_____

MORE ON BACK ▶
• Complete all applicable spaces (numbers 5-9) on the reverse side of this page.
• See detailed instructions.
• Sign the form at line 8.

DO NOT WRITE HERE

	FORM VA
EXAMINED BY	
CHECKED BY	
CORRESPONDENCE ☐ Yes	FOR COPYRIGHT OFFICE USE ONLY

DO NOT WRITE ABOVE THIS LINE. IF YOU NEED MORE SPACE, USE A SEPARATE CONTINUATION SHEET.

PREVIOUS REGISTRATION Has registration for this work, or for an earlier version of this work, already been made in the Copyright Office?
☐ Yes ☐ No   If your answer is "Yes," why is another registration being sought? (Check appropriate box.)
a. ☐ This is the first published edition of a work previously registered in unpublished form.
b. ☐ This is the first application submitted by this author as copyright claimant.
c. ☐ This is a changed version of the work, as shown by space 6 on this application.
If your answer is "Yes," give: Previous Registration Number ▼   Year of Registration ▼

5

DERIVATIVE WORK OR COMPILATION Complete both space 6a and 6b for a derivative work; complete only 6b for a compilation.
Preexisting Material Identify any preexisting work or works that this work is based on or incorporates. ▼

a

6

Material Added to This Work Give a brief, general statement of the material that has been added to this work and in which copyright is claimed. ▼

See instructions before completing this space.

b

DEPOSIT ACCOUNT If the registration fee is to be charged to a Deposit Account established in the Copyright Office, give name and number of Account.
Name ▼   Account Number ▼

a

7

CORRESPONDENCE Give name and address to which correspondence about this application should be sent. Name/Address/Apt/City/State/Zip ▼

b

Area code and daytime telephone number ▶   Fax number ▶
Email ▶

CERTIFICATION* I, the undersigned, hereby certify that I am the
Check only one ☐ author
☐ other copyright claimant
☐ owner of exclusive right(s)
☐ authorized agent of _____
Name of author or other copyright claimant, or owner of exclusive right(s) ▲
of the work identified in this application and that the statements made by me in this application are correct to the best of my knowledge.

8

Typed or printed name and date ▼ If this application gives a date of publication in space 3, do not sign and submit it before that date.

_____   Date ▶ _____

Hand written signature ▼

X _____

Certificate will be mailed in window envelope to this address:	Name ▼	**YOU MUST:** • Complete all necessary spaces • Sign your application in space 8 **SEND ALL 3 ELEMENTS IN THE SAME PACKAGE** 1. Application form 2. Nonrefundable filling fee in chuck or money order payable to *Register of Copyrights* 3. Deposit material **MAIL TO:** Library of Congress Copyright Office 101 Independence Avenue SE Washington. DC 20559
	Number/Street/Apt ▼	
	City/State/Zip ▼	

9

*17 USC §506(8): Any person who knowingly makes a false representation of a material fact in the application for copyright registration provided for by section 409, or in any written statement filed in connection with the application, shall be fined not more than $2,500.
Form TX — Full Rev:05/2012 Print 05/2012 – 8,000 Printed on recycled paper   U.S. Government Printing Office: 2012-372-482/80,911

TRADEMARKS

Trademarks offer another form of protection pursuant to the laws of the United States. It consists of any name, symbol, device or combination thereof used to identify and distinguish one's goods....from those manufactured or sold by others; and to indicate the source of such goods.

Its protections are governed under both federal and state law, and protects registered works as well as qualifying unregistered works.

The strength of a mark dictates the level of protection it receives and is a vital consideration in determining the scope of protection it should be accorded.

However, contrary to copyrights, a business does not necessarily obtain a protective interest in a mark simply by using it to represent its services; and a business will obtain rights to the mark upon first use only if the mark is "inherently distinctive."

The concept of descriptiveness must be construed rather broadly. Whenever a word or phrase naturally directs attention to the qualities, characteristics, effect or purpose of the product or service, it is descriptive and cannot be infringed upon.

Pursuant to the "Lanham Act" 15 U.S.C. §1114 courts have looked to three factors in determining the protection of a trademark: (1) the distinctiveness of the mark; (2) whether the mark has been declared as "Incontestable" under 15 U.S.C. §1065(3); and (3) the extent of third party use of the mark.

The distinctiveness of a mark has been characterized as its tendency to identify the goods sold under the mark as emanating from a particular, although possibly anonymous source. By this, there are four categories of distinctiveness: (1)generic; (2) descriptive; (3) suggestive; and (4)arbitrary, with generic being the weakest and arbitrary being the strongest.

Lets start first with generic. A generic mark is one which suggests the basic nature of service and is typically incapable of achieving service mark protection because it has no distinctiveness.

Descriptive: a descriptive mark identifies a characteristic or quality of a service and, because such a mark is not inherently distinctive, it may be protected only if it acquires a secondary meaning.

Suggestive: a suggestive mark suggests the characteristics of the service and requires an effort of the imagination by the consumer in order to be understood as descriptive. No proof of a secondary meaning is required for the mark to be protected under this prong.

Arbitrary: an arbitrary or fanciful mark is also inherently distinctive because the term bears no relationship to the service and is thus protected without proof of a secondary meaning as well.

In determining incontestability, courts look to the first use of the mark in connection with its services, when was those services used in commerce and when was the mark established.

When finally looking to third party use of the mark, the courts ruled that the less third parties use a mark, the stronger such mark becomes and the more protection it deserves. Therefore, if the name, symbol or mark is so distinct that it can in no way be used by third parties then the stronger the trademark protection appears pursuant to the "Lanham Act."

SERVICE MARKS

Service Marks however, are just the same as Trademarks except for the fact that service marks are specifically business names or words that identify and distinguish the unique service, from the service of others. In all other contexts, everything applies as it does in trademark determinations.

INFRINGEMENT FEES

Under the "Lanham Act" 15 U.S.C. §1114 (1), a defendant is liable for infringement; if, without consent, he or she uses any reproduction, counterfeit, copy, or colorable imitation of a registered mark "which is likely to cause confusion, mistake or deception."

For counterfeit trademarks or service mark violations, the court may award an amount of no less than $500 dollars but no more than $100,000 dollars per counterfeit mark **per type of good or service sold.** 15 U.S.C. §1117(c) (1).

The court may, as it considers just, award as much as $1,000,000 dollars per counterfeit mark **per type of good or service sold** if it finds the use of the counterfeit mark to be willful. 15 U.S.C. §1117(c)(2).

DURATION Of TRADEMARK/SERVICE MARK

The duration of trademark ownership "initially" last for twenty (20) years; and every ten (10) years afterwards, unless previously cancelled or surrendered.

However, the application for renewal must be filed within one year before the expiration date of registration; or within the six month grace period after the expiration date of registration.

If no renewal application is filed within either period, the registration will expire and ownership will be surrendered and abandoned.

ESTABLISHING FIRST USE

Establishing first use pursuant to the standards of The United States Trademark and Patent Office, requires the owner of the mark to:
 a. Use the mark, logo, name, word, brand on or in connection with the goods or services of the public;
 b. That such use of the mark has to be proven to have been used **also** in commerce; when on or in connection with such goods or services **(a quick secret to using the mark in commerce is to establish a website and post the mark on its page);**

c. That the owner of said mark submit one specimen showing how the mark was actually used on the product in commerce. For example: if you had a logo for an apparel line, then you would submit a photo of a t-shirt bearing the mark. Or if you had a business name for a shipping service, you would submit a picture of a shipping package bearing the mark.

POOR MAN'S PROOF

Forget about what you heard about placing your evidenced of 'first use' documents in an envelope and mailing it back to yourself and not opening it. Although it works its just not as sure fire as the secret I'm about to share with you; and what I'm about to spill could make people mad at you and me. However, I haven't heard of it being illegal; and should it later become prohibited to the extent of illegal, then go back to the poor man's way. Meanwhile, pay close attention:

First you will need to abide by all requirements on the applications you file. Then mail the application, and a copy, to either the Library of Congress or The United States Patent and Trademark Office. Do not include any funds.

When either office receive said applications staff will automatically stamp the documents received on that date. When this happens they would immediately notice that no payment was included and subsequently mail you back a notice indicating the absence of payment, along with a copy of your application with the file date stamped across it.

At this point, you don't need to pay, because the date that the application was received by the office is evidence that your work was submitted to that office on said date; and anyone whom later claims ownership to such marks or copyrights will have to produce 'first use' prior to the date on your records.

Neat hunh? Well don't ask me how long will this last.

TRADEMARK & SERVICE MARK FEES

At press time of this book, the United States Patent and Trademark Office fees were $375 dollars in U.S. currency, paid via United States Postal Money Order or credit card only (no personal or cashiers checks).

AMENDMENTS AND ADDITIONAL FEES

To use the same name of your mark, word, logo, etc. but with a variety of other designs different from the original mark, word, logo etc. that you initially submitted to the USPTO, Then you are required to submit the different mark, word, logo, etc. and $100 dollars for every different mark, word, logo, etc. thereafter.

For Example: If I submitted a mark under graphics. After the initial registration fee is paid, I will then be required to submit $100 dollars with every different mark I wanted to register under that mark there afterwards.

LIST OF GOODS

Followed are a list of goods and services that must be selected as the class of goods which falls within its said category. For example, if you wanted to use your mark, word, logo etc., in connection with watches, then your class of goods selected would be "27 U.S./14 International."

If more than one item of goods and services is specified in the application, then the dates of use, along with a "specimen" is needed to be submitted for each class. In such case additional registration fees are needed.
Each specific class of services intended to be used, mandates a registration fee of its own.

HOW TO SECURE YOUR OWN TRADEMARK/SERVICE MARK

Securing a Trademark or Service Mark is much easier than it sounds; and it can be done without the aide of counsel, despite counsel selling you all types of rubbish on the strict criterias it takes to rightfully secure said marks. Follow the rules and guidelines below and registering a Trademark and or Service Mark will become easy as the names, words and or logos you come up with.

First you have to write a letter to The United States Patent and Trademark Office and request a registration form. The address is:
United States Patent and Trademark Office

600 Dulany Street
Alexandria, Virginia
22314-5193

Once you receive the form you will complete the following process:
   a. State the name of the applicant;
   b. State the citizenship of the applicant;
   c. State whether applicant is a corporation, association, person, etc.;
   d. State whether applicant is a partnership, limited partnership, etc.;
   e. State applicant's address;
   f. State the list of particular goods or services for which the mark, word, logo, etc. may be used;
   g. State the International class of goods or services;
   h. Submit a description of the mark;
   i. List a "verified Statement" paragraph, stating that the translation of the mark if the mark is not in english; or stating that the mark has no meaning in english if it appears foreign;
   j. Stating a "Basis for Filing" Follow below:

List a short paragraph stating that pursuant to 1 (a) of the Act, all requirements are met.
   1. That the applicant's first use of the mark, word, logo, etc., on or in connection with the listed goods and or services was **(give date);**
   2. That the applicant's first use of the mark, word, logo, etc., in commerce as a trademark or service mark was **(give date);**
   3. That the applicant has submitted at least "one specimen" showing how the applicant actually uses the mark, word, logo, etc. in commerce **(submit photo);**

Remember, if more than one item of goods or services is specified in the application, the dates of use in each class is mandated.

   k. Submit a drawing of the mark (follow instructions below):

The drawing must show only one clear mark.

Applicants whom seek to register words, letters, numbers or any combination thereof without claim to any particular font style, size or color, must submit a standard character drawing that shows the mark in **"BLACK"** on a "WHITE" background.

This method should state that the mark, word, logo etc., is in standard characters and no claim is made to any particular font style, size or color.

Applicants whom seek to register a mark, word, logo, etc. that includes a "two or three" dimensional design, color and or words, letters, numbers, etc. or the combination thereof, in a particular font style, or size must submit a special drawing, showing the mark, word, logo, etc. in color; and the applicant must name the specific colors in its specific spaces on or in the mark, word, logo, etc. The applicant must also submit a "verified Statement" that the color(s) are features of the mark, word, logo, etc.; and a black and white drawing of the mark, word, logo, etc. must be submitted as well.

Three dimensional marks with colors should have a claim that the mark is three dimensional. One must be black and white with the colors stated; and one must be three dimensional with the colors shown in it.

MOTION MARKS

If the mark have motion, the drawing should depict a single point in the movement, or the drawing should depict up to five freeze frames showing various points in the movement, whichever best depicts the commercial impression of the mark, word, logo, etc.

The applicant must also describe the mark, word, logo, etc.

DIGITAL IMAGES

The requirement for digital images must be in ".jpgx" format and scanned at no less than 300 dots per inch and no more than 350 dots per inch with a length and width of no less than 250 pixels and no more than 944 pixels. All lines must be clean, sharp and solid; not fined or crowded, and produce a high quality image when copied.

PAPER SIZE

The paper size requirements are 8 to 8.5 inches (20.3 to 21.6 cm) wide, and 11 to 11.69 inches (27.9 to 29.7 cm) long.

One of the shorter sides of the sheet should be regarded as its top edge. The image must be no larger than 3.15 inches (8cm) high by 3.15 inches (8cm) wide.

Include in the caption "DRAWING PAGE" at the top of the drawing, beginning one inch (25cm) from the top edge; and the drawing must be typed or made with a pen, or by a process that will provide high definition when copied.

However, a photo lithograph, printer's proof copy, or other high quality reproduction of the mark may be used.
All lines must be clean, sharp and solid; and must not be fine or crowded.

SPECIMEN

A trademark specimen is a label, tag, or container for the goods; or a display associated with the goods. The office may accept another document related to the goods or the sale of the goods when it is impracticable to place the mark on the goods, packaging for the goods, or displays associated with the goods.

A Service Mark specimen must show the mark, word, logo, etc., as actually used in the sale or advertising of the services.

A photocopy or other reproduction of a specimen of the mark as actually used on or in connection with the goods, or in the sale or advertising of the services is acceptable.

The specimen should be flat, and not larger than 8½ inches (21.6 cm) wide, by 11.69 inches (29.7cm) long. If a specimen of this size is not available, the applicant may substitute a suitable photograph or other facsimile.

TRADEMARK INFRINGEMENT FEES

The Lanham Act permits statutory damages for service mark and trademark infringements. 15 U.S.C. §1117(a)

The court will award the maximum amount available, which is $2,000,000 dollars when the court finds that use of the marks, words, logos, etc. was willful. 15 U.S.C. §1117(c)(2).

Followed is a schedule of classes of Goods and Services for U.S. Trademarks. The actual U.S. Trademarks application can be found in 'X Marks the Spot.'

PART 6 -- CLASSIFICATION OF GOODS AND SERVICES UNDER THE TRADEMARK ACT

§ 6.1 International schedule of classes of goods and services.

Goods

1. Chemicals used in industry, science and photography, as well as in agriculture, horticulture and forestry; unprocessed artificial resins, unprocessed plastics; manures; fee extinguishing compositions; tempering and soldering preparations; chemical substances for preserving foodstuffs; tanning substances; adhesives used in industry.

2. Paints, varnishes, lacquers; preservatives against rust and against deterioration of wood; colorants; mordants; raw natural resins; metals in foil and powder form for painters, decorators, printers and artists.

3. Bleaching preparations and other substances for laundry use; cleaning, polishing, scouring and abrasive preparations; soaps; perfumery, essential oils, cosmetics, hair lotions; dentifrices.

4. Industrial oils and greases; lubricants; dust absorbing, wetting and binding compositions; fuels (including motor spirit) and illuminants; candles and wicks for lighting.

5. Pharmaceutical and veterinary preparations; sanitary preparations for medical purposes; dietetic substances adapted for medical use, food

for babies; plasters, materials for dressings; material for stopping teeth, dental wax; disinfectants; preparations for destroying vermin; fungicides, herbicides.

6. Common metals and their alloys; metal building materials; transportable buildings of metal; materials of metal for railway tracks; non-electric cables and wires of common metal; ironmongery, small items of metal hardware; pipes and tubes of metal; safes; goods of common metal not included in other classes; ores.

7. Machines and machine tools; motors and engines (except for land vehicles); machine coupling and transmission components (except for land vehicles); agricultural-implements other than hand-operated; incubators for eggs.

8. Hand tools and implements (hand-operated); cutlery; side arms; razors.

9. Scientific, nautical, surveying, photographic, cinematographic, optical, weighing, measuring, signalling, checking (supervision), life-saving and teaching apparatus and instruments; apparatus and instruments for conducting, switching, transforming, accumulating, regulating or controlling electricity; apparatus for recording, transmission or reproduction of sound or images; magnetic data carriers, recording discs; automatic vending machines and mechanisms for coin-operated apparatus; cash registers, calculating machines, data processing equipment and computers; fire-extinguishing apparatus.

10. Surgical, medical, dental and veterinary apparatus and instruments, artificial limbs, eyes and teeth; orthopedic articles; suture materials.

11. Apparatus for lighting, heating, steam generating, cooking, refrigerating, drying, ventilating, water supply and sanitary purposes.

12. Vehicles; apparatus for locomotion by land, air or water.

13. Firearms; ammunition and projectiles; explosives; fireworks.

14. Precious metals and their alloys and goods in precious metals or coated therewith, not included in other classes; jewellery, precious stones; horological and chronometric instruments.

15. Musical instruments.

16. Paper, cardboard and goods made from these materials, not included in other classes; printed matter; bookbinding material; photographs; stationery; adhesives for stationery or household purposes; artists' materials; paint brushes; typewriters and office requisites (except furniture); instructional and teaching material (except apparatus); plastic materials for packaging (not included in other classes); printers' type; printing blocks.

17. Rubber, gutta-percha, gum, asbestos, mica and goods made from these materials and not included in other classes; plastics in extruded form for use in manufacture; packing, stopping and insulating materials; flexible pipes, not of metal.

18. Leather and imitations of leather, and goods made of these materials and not included in other classes; animal skins, hides; trunks and travelling bags; umbrellas, parasols and walking sticks; whips, harness and saddlery.

19. Building materials (non-metallic); non-metallic rigid pipes for building; asphalt, pitch and bitumen; non-metallic transportable buildings; monuments, not of metal.

20. Furniture, mirrors, picture frames; goods (not included in other classes) of wood, cork, reed, cane, wicker, horn, bone, ivory, whalebone, shell, amber, mother-of-pearl, meerschaum and substitutes for all these materials, or of plastics.

21. Household or kitchen utensils and containers; combs and sponges; brushes (except paint brushes); brush-making materials; articles for cleaning purposes; steelwool; unworked or semi-worked glass (except glass used in building); glassware, porcelain and earthenware not included in other classes.

22. Ropes, string, nets, tents, awnings, tarpaulins, sails, sacks and bags (not included in other classes); padding and stuffing materials (except of rubber or plastics); raw fibrous textile materials.

23. Yarns and threads, for textile use.

24. Textiles and textile goods, not included in other classes; bed and table covers.
25. Clothing, footwear, headgear.
26. Lace and embroidery, ribbons and braid; buttons, hooks and eyes, pins and needles; artificial flowers.
27. Carpets, rugs, mats and matting, linoleum and other materials for covering existing floors; wall hangings (non-textile).
28. Games and playthings; gymnastic and sporting articles not included in other classes; decorations for Christmas trees.
29. Meat, fish, poultry and game; meat extracts; preserved, frozen, dried and cooked fruits and vegetables; jellies, jams, compotes; eggs, milk and milk products; edible oils and fats.
30. Coffee, tea, cocoa, sugar, rice, tapioca, sago, artificial coffee; flour and preparations made from cereals, bread, pastry and confectionery, ices; honey, treacle; yeast, baking-powder; salt, mustard; vinegar, sauces (condiments); spices; ice.
31. Agricultural, horticultural and forestry products and grains not included in other classes; live animals; fresh fruits and vegetables; seeds, natural plants and flowers; foodstuffs for animals, malt.
32. Beers; mineral and aerated waters and other non-alcoholic drinks; fruit drinks and fruit juices; syrups and other preparations for making beverages.
33. Alcoholic beverages (except beers).
34. Tobacco; smokers' articles; matches.

Services

35. Advertising; business management; business administration; office functions.
36. Insurance; financial affairs; monetary affairs; real estate affairs.
37. Building construction; repair; installation services.
38. Telecommunications.

39. Transport; packaging and storage of goods; travel arrangement.

40. Treatment of materials.

41. Education; providing of training; entertainment; sporting and cultural activities.

42. Scientific and technological services and research and design relating thereto; industrial analysis and research services; design and development of computer hardware and software.

43. Services for providing food and drink; temporary accommodation.

44. Medical services; veterinary services; hygienic and beauty care for human beings or animals; agriculture, horticulture and forestry services.

45. Legal services; security services for the protection of property and individuals; personal and social services rendered by others to meet the needs of individuals.

[38 FR 14681, June 4, 1973; 64 FR 48900, 48927, Sept. 8, 1999; 66 FR 48338, 48339, Sept. 20, 2001; 72 FR 28610, 28611, May 22, 2007]

Sees. 30, 41, 60 Stat. 436, 440; 15 U.S.C. 1112, 1123.

[EFFECTIVE DATE NOTE: 72 FR 28610, 28611, May 22, 2007, revised this section, effective May 22, 2007.]

§ 6.2 Prior U.S. schedule of classes of goods and services.

Class	Title
	Goods
1	Raw or partly prepared materials.
2	Receptacles.
3	Baggage, animal equipments, portfolios, and pocket books.
4	Abrasives and polishing materials.
5	Adhesives.
6	Chemicals and chemical compositions.
7	Cordage.
8	Smokers' articles, not including tobacco products.
9	Explosives, firearms, equipments, and projectiles.
10	Fertilizers.
11	Inks and inking materials.
12	Construction materials.
13	Hardware and plumbing and steamfitting supplies.
14	Metals and metal castings and forgings.
15	Oils and greases.
16	Protective and decorative coatings.
17	Tobacco products.
18	Medicines and pharmaceutical preparations.
19	Vehicles.
20	Linoleum and oiled cloth.
21	Electrical apparatus, machines, and supplies.
22	Games, toys, and sporting goods.
23	Cutlery, machinery, and tools, and parts thereof.
24	Laundry appliances and machines.
25	Locks and safes.
26	Measuring and scientific appliances.
27	Horological instruments.
28	Jewelry and precious-metal ware.
29	Brooms, brushes, and dusters.
30	Crockery, earthenware, and porcelain.
31	Filters and refrigerators.
32	Furniture and upholstery.
33	Glassware.

34	Heating, lighting, and ventilating apparatus.
35	Belting, hose, machinery packing, and nonmetallic tires.
36	Musical instruments and supplies.
37	Paper and stationery.
38	Prints and publications.
39	Clothing.
40	Fancy goods, furnishings, and notions.
41	Canes, parasols, and umbrellas.
42	Knitted, netted, and textile fabrics, and substitutes therefor.
43	Thread and yarn.
44	Dental, medical, and surgical appliances.
45	Soft drinks and carbonated waters.
46	Foods and ingredients of foods.
47	Wines.
48	Malt beverages and liquors.
49	Distilled alcoholic liquors.
50	Merchandise not otherwise classified.
51	Cosmetics and toilet preparations.
52	Detergents and soaps.

Services

100	Miscellaneous.
101	Advertising and business.
102	Insurance and financial.
103	Construction and repair.
104	Communication.
105	Transportation and storage.
106	Material treatment.
107	Education and entertainment.

[24 FR 10383, Dec. 22, 1959. Redesignated at 38 FR 14681, June 4, 1973]

Sees. 30, 41, 60 Stat. 436, 440; 15 U.S.C. 1112, 1123.

STATE TRADEMARKS

There's another type of trademark that you should also be familiar with. It is afforded the same protections that is afforded the U.S. trademark, although the only difference is the duration protection period. It is known as the 'State Trademark.'

The difference between the two is that the U.S. Trademark offers trademark protections throughout the entire United States, while the State Trademark offers trademark protections throughout your state only. Also, the state trademark application fee is $87.50 and the duration period is only five years, then it has to be renewed.

I have also supplied a state trademark application form for Florida. Remember, if you are not from there, then find your state online website in Chapter 5 and fill out a form. It basically has the same language as the Florida form.

TRADEMARK/SERVICE MARK REGISTRATION GUIDELINES

I. GENERAL INFORMATION

Trademarks and Service Marks may be registered with the Florida Department of State pursuant to Chapter 495, Florida Statutes. Registration must be denied if a mark does not meet and comply with all of the requirements and provisions stipulated in Chapter 495, Florida Statutes. Marks are checked against other marks registered with this division and not against corporations, fictitious names or other entities. Rights to a name or mark are perfected by actual use in the ordinary pursuit of the specific endeavor; rights are not perfected by registration only, and the general rule of "FIRST IN USE, FIRST IN RIGHT" is applicable.

Our agency registers trade and service marks on a state level. If you need information concerning the federal registration of trademarks, service marks or patents, please contact the Commissioner of Patents and Trademarks in Washington, D. C. by calling 571-272-1000. If you need information concerning copyrights, contact the Copyright Office in Washington, D.

C. by calling 202-707-3000. Although trade names are defined in Chapter 495, Florida Statutes, there is no provision for their registration.

If you wish to register a mark pursuant to Chapter 495, Florida Statutes, please submit one original and one photocopy of the Trade or Service Mark Registration application completed in its entirety, three specimens and a check made payable to the Florida Department of State for the appropriate amount. The application must be typed or neatly handwritten, signed and notarized.

The mark must be in use before it can be registered. If registering a trademark, the good(s) or product(s) must be on sale in the market place. If registering a service mark, you must be rendering the service(s) you are advertising. The mere advertising of future goods or services does not constitute use of a trade or service mark.

II. FEES AND CLASSES

The fee to register a mark is $87.50 per class. Please refer to section 495.111, Florida Statutes (attached), for a list of classes. A certificate of registration will be issued free of charge. Please make check payable to the Florida Department of State.

Should you need additional information concerning these classes or your classification, please contact the Registration Section by calling (850)245-6051.

III. SPECIMENS (SAMPLES)

You must submit three specimens (samples) showing how the mark is used. They may be originals or legible facsimiles (copies).

If your mark is a trademark, we will need specimens that are affixed to the good(s) or product(s). Some acceptable trademark specimens are: labels, decals, tags, wrappers, boxes, and containers. If your mark is a service mark, we will need specimens which reflect the type of service(s) being provided. Some acceptable service mark specimens are: business cards, brochures, flyers, and newspaper advertisements.

If your mark is both a trade and service mark, you must submit three appropriate trademark specimens and three appropriate service mark specimens.

Do not submit camera-ready copies, letterhead stationery, envelopes, invoices or matchbooks as specimens. Photographs of bulky specimens are acceptable if the mark to be registered and the good(s) or product(s) are clearly legible. We will not accept any specimens that have been altered or defaced in any way.

IV. APPLICATION

Part I

#1 - You must list the complete name and business address of the applicant. Please indicate if the applicant is an individual, a corporation, a limited partnership, a general partnership, etc. Enter the domicile state, Florida registration number and Federal Employer Identification number if the applicant is other than an individual.

#2(a) - If a service mark, list the services the mark is used in connection with (i.e., restaurant services, real estate agency, insurance agency, etc.).

#2(b) - If a trademark, list the goods/products the mark is used in connection with (i.e., window cleaner, furniture polish, ladies sportswear, etc.).

#2(c) - List the specific way the mark is applied to the good(s) or used in advertising: If a trademark, tell how the mark is applied to the goods (i.e., label, decal, engraving, imprinting on the goods or products themselves, etc.).

If a service mark, tell how the mark is used in advertising (i.e., brochures, business cards, newspaper advertisements, etc.).

#2(d) - List the applicable class(es). Please refer to section 495.111, F.S., (attached) for a list of these classes.

Part II

#1(a) - Enter the date the mark was first used anywhere.
#1(b) - Enter the date the mark was first used in Florida.

Part III

#1 - Enter the mark to be registered. If the mark includes a design, include a brief written description. If your mark is in another language, please provide this office with an English translation of your mark in this section.

#2 - Disclaimer - Your mark may include a word or design that must be disclaimed. All geographical terms and representations of cities, states or countries must be disclaimed (i.e., Miami, Orlando, Florida, the design of the state of Florida, the design of the United States of America, etc.). Commonly used words, including corporate suffixes, must also be disclaimed.

Signature Portion

Complete the signature paragraph accordingly. Please note the applicant's signature must be notarized.

V. TRADEMARK/SERVICE MARK SEARCH

Due to the amount of time it takes to conduct a thorough search of the records, this office does not provide trademark/service mark searches over the telephone. However, you may submit a written request. The request must specify the exact mark to be used and the good(s) or service(s) the mark is to be used in connection with. Please direct all requests to the Trademark Registration Section, Division of Corporations, P. O. Box 6327, Tallahassee, FL 32314.

VI. PROCESSING TIME

The application should be processed within two to five business days from the date of receipt. The processing time may be longer during our peak periods. All applications meeting the requirements of Chapter 495, F. S., on the initial examination will be filed as of the date of receipt. Applications received by courier are not handled on an expedited basis.

VII. COURIER ADDRESS AND MAILING ADDRESS

Mailing Address	Street/Courier Address
Registration Section	Registration Section
Division of Corporations	Division of Corporations
P.O. Box 6327	Clifton Building
Tallahassee, FL 32314	2661 Executive Center Circle Tallahassee, FL 32301

<u>Applications received via a courier service are not handled on an expedited basis.</u>

VIII. QUESTIONS

If you have any questions concerning the registration of a mark, please contact the Trademark Registration Section by calling (850)245-6051 between the hours of 8 a.m. and 5:00 p.m. or writing to an address listed above.

495.111 Classification.--

(1) The following general classes of goods and services, conforming to the classification adopted by the United States Patent and Trademark Office, are established for convenience of administration of this chapter:

(a) Goods:

1. Class 1 Chemicals used in industry, science, and photography; agriculture, horticulture, and forestry; unprocessed artificial resins, unprocessed plastics; manures; fire extinguishing compositions; tempering and soldering preparations; chemical substances for preserving foodstuffs; tanning substances; and adhesives used in industry.

2. Class 2 Paints, varnishes, lacquers; preservatives against rust and against deterioration of wood; colorants; mordants; raw natural resins; and metals in foil and powder form for painters, decorators, printers, and artists.

3. Class 3 Bleaching preparations and other substances for laundry use; cleaning, polishing, scouring, and abrasive preparations; soaps; perfumery, essential oils, cosmetics, and hair lotions; and dentifrices.

4. Class 4 Industrial oils and greases; lubricants; dust absorbing, wetting, and binding compositions; fuels (including motor spirit) and illuminants; and candles and wicks for lighting.

5. Class 5 Pharmaceuticals and veterinary preparations; sanitary preparations for medical purposes; dietetic substances adapted for medical use and food for babies; plasters and materials for dressings; material for stopping teeth and dental wax; disinfectants; preparations for destroying vermin; and fungicides and herbicides.

6. Class 6 Common metals and their alloys; metal building materials; transportable buildings of metal; materials of metal for railway tracks; nonelectric cables and wires of common metal; ironmongery and small items of metal hardware; pipes and tubes of metal; safes; goods of common metal not included in other classes; and ores.

7. Class 7 Machines and machine tools; motors and engines (except for land vehicles); machine coupling and transmission components (except for land vehicles); agricultural implements other than hand-operated; incubators for eggs.

8. Class 8 Hand tools and hand-operated implements; cutlery; side arms; and razors.

9. Class 9 Scientific, nautical, surveying, photographic, cinematographic, optical, weighing, measuring, signaling, checking (supervision), and life-saving and teaching apparatus and instruments; apparatus and instruments for conducting, switching, transforming, accumulating, regulating, or controlling electricity; apparatus for recording, transmission, or reproduction of sound or images; magnetic data carriers and recording discs; automatic vending machines and mechanisms for coin-operated apparatus; cash registers, calculating machines, and data processing equipment and computers; and fire-extinguishing apparatus.

10. Class 10 Surgical, medical, dental, and veterinary apparatus and instruments, artificial limbs, eyes, and teeth; orthopedic articles; and suture materials.

11. Class 11 Apparatus for lighting, heating, steam generating, cooking, refrigerating, drying, ventilating, water supply, and sanitary purposes.

12. Class 12 Vehicles; apparatus for locomotion by land, air, or water.

13. Class 13 Firearms; ammunition and projectiles; explosives; and fireworks.

14. Class 14 Precious metals and their alloys and goods in precious metals or coated therewith (not included in other classes); jewelry and precious stones; and horological and chronometric instruments.

15. Class 15 Musical instruments.

16. Class 16 Paper, cardboard, and goods made from these materials (not included in other classes); printed matter; bookbinding material; photographs; stationery; adhesives for stationery or household purposes; artists' materials; paint brushes; typewriters and office requisites (except furniture); instructional and teaching material (except apparatus); plastic materials for packaging (not included in other classes); printers' type; and printing blocks.

17. Class 17 Rubber, gutta-percha, gum, asbestos, mica, and goods made from these materials and not included in other classes; plastics in extruded form for use in manufacture; packing, stopping, and insulating materials; and flexible pipes not of metal.

18. Class 18 Leather and imitations of leather and goods made of these materials and not included in other classes; animal skins and hides; trunks and traveling bags; umbrellas, parasols, and walking sticks; and whips, harness, and saddlery.

19. Class 19 Building materials (nonmetallic); nonmetailic rigid pipes for building; asphalt, pitch, and bitumen; nonmetallic transportable buildings; monuments, not of metal.

20. Class 20 Furniture, mirrors, and picture frames; goods (not included in other classes) of wood, cork, reed, cane, wicker, horn, bone, ivory, whalebone, shell, amber, mother-of-pearl, and meerschaum and substitutes for all these materials, or of plastics.

21. Class 21 Household or kitchen utensils and containers (not of precious metal or coated therewith); combs and sponges; brushes (except paint brushes); brush-making materials; articles for cleaning purposes; steel wool; unworked or semiworked glass (except glass used in building); and glassware, porcelain, and earthenware not included in other classes.

22. Class 22 Ropes, string, nets, tents, awnings, tarpaulins, sails, sacks, and bags (not included in other classes); padding and stuffing materials (except of rubber or plastics); and raw fibrous textile materials.

23. Class 23 Yarns and threads for textile use.

24. Class 24 Textiles and textile goods not included in other classes and bed and table covers.

25. Class 25 Clothing, footwear, and headgear.
26. Class 26 Lace and embroidery, ribbons, and braid; buttons, hooks and eyes, pins, and needles; and artificial flowers.
27. Class 27 Carpets, rugs, mats and matting, linoleum, and other materials for covering existing floors; and wall hangings (nontextile).
28. Class 28 Games and playthings; gymnastic and sporting articles not included in other classes; and decorations for Christmas trees.
29. Class 29 Meat, fish, poultry, and game; meat extracts; preserved, dried, and cooked fruits and vegetables; jellies, jams, and compotes; eggs, milk, and milk products; and edible oils and fats.
30. Class 30 Coffee, tea, cocoa, sugar, rice, tapioca, sago, and artificial coffee; flour and preparations made from cereals, bread, pastry and confectionery, and ices; honey and treacle; yeast, baking powder; salt, and mustard; vinegar and sauces (condiments); spices; and ice.
31. Class 31 Agricultural, horticultural, and forestry products and grains not included in other classes; live animals; fresh fruits and vegetables; seeds, natural plants, and flowers; foodstuffs for animals and malt.
32. Class 32 Beers; mineral and aerated waters and other nonalcoholic drinks; fruit drinks and fruit juices; and syrups and other preparations for making beverages.
33. Class 33 Alcoholic beverages except beers.
34. Class 34 Tobacco; smokers' articles; and matches.

(b) Services:

1. Class 35 Advertising; business management; business administration; and office functions.
2. Class 36 Insurance; financial affairs; monetary affairs; and real estate affairs.
3. Class 37 Building construction; repair; and installation services.
4. Class 38 Telecommunications.
5. Class 39 Transport; packaging and storage of goods; and travel arrangements.

6. Class 40 Treatment of materials.
7. Class 41 Education; providing of training; entertainment; and sporting and cultural activities.
8. Class 42 Scientific and technological services and research and design relating thereto; industrial analysis and research services; design and development of computer hardware and software; and legal services.
9. Class 43 Services for providing food and drink; and temporary accommodation.
10. Class 44 Medical services; veterinary services; hygienic and beauty care for human beings or animals; and agriculture, horticulture, and forestry services.
11. Class 45 Personal and social services rendered by others to meet the needs of individuals; and security services for the protection of property and individuals.

(c) **Certification and collective membership marks:**
1. Class 200 Collective membership marks.
2. Class A Certification marks for goods.
3. Class B Certification marks for services.

(d) **The goods and services recited in collective trademark and collective service mark applications are assigned to the same classes that are appropriate for those goods and services in general.**

(2) The establishment of the classes of goods and services set forth in subsection (1) is not for the purpose of limiting or extending the rights of the applicant or registrant. A single application for registration of a mark may include any or all goods upon which, or services with which, the mark is actually being used comprised in one or more of the classes listed, but in the event that a single application includes goods or services in connection with which the mark is being used which fall within different classes of goods or services, a fee equaling the sum of the fees for registration in each class shall be payable.

COVER LETTER

TO: Registration Section
Division of Corporations

SUBJECT: _____
(Mark to be registered)

The enclosed Trademark/Service Mark Application, specimens and fee(s) are submitted for filing.

Please return all correspondence concerning this matter to the following:

_____
(Name of Person)

_____
(Firm/Company)

_____
(Address)

_____
(City/State and Zip Code)

For further information concerning this matter, please call:

_____ at (_____) _____
(Name of Person)   (Area Code & Daytime Telephone Number)

MAILING ADDRESS:
Registration Section
Division of Corporations
P.O. Box 6327
Tallahassee, FL 32314

STREET/COURIER ADDRESS:
Registration Section
Division of Corporations
Clifton Building
2661 Executive Center Circle
Tallahassee, FL 32301

(NOTE: The information contained in this cover letter will be included in the permanent record and will be available to the general public.)

APPLICATION FOR THE REGISTRATION OF A TRADEMARK OR SERVICE MARK
Pursuant to Chapter 495, Florida Statutes

TO: Division of Corporations
Post Office Box 6327
Tallahassee, FL 32314

PART I

1. OWNER/APPLICANT: Enter the name and address of the individual or the business entity to be listed as the owner of the Trademark and/or Service Mark on the records of the Florida Department of State.

(a) Owner's/Applicant's name: _____

(b) Owner's/Applicant's business address: _____

City/State/Zip

If different, Owner's/Applicant's mailing address: _____

City/State/Zip

(c) Owner's/Applicant's telephone number: _____

Check the appropriate box to indicate the Owner/Applicant is a(n):

☐ Individual   ☐ Corporation   ☐ Joint Venture   ☐ Limited Liability Company
☐ General Partnership   ☐ Limited Partnership   ☐ Union   ☐ Other: _____

If the Owner/Applicant is a business entity, the business entity must have an active filing or registration on file with the Florida Department of State. If the Owner/Applicant is <u>not</u> an individual, enter the business entity's Florida registration/document number in #1, the state or country under the laws of which the business entity is currently formed, organized or incorporated under in #2, and the entity's federal employer identification number (EM) in #3.

(1) Florida registration/document number: _____

(2) Domicile State or Country: _____

(3) Federal Employer Identification Number: _____

2. (a) <u>SERVICE MARK:</u> If the owner/applicant is using the name, logo, design and/or slogan being registered in connection with a type of service, the mark is a service mark. If the mark is a service mark, the applicant/owner must list the specific service(s) the mark is being used in connection with. For example: furniture moving services, diaper services, house painting services, wholesale and retail sales of tractor equipment, etc. <u>If the owner/applicant is using the mark to identify services available in the market place, enter the specific service(s) being rendered here:</u>

(Note: List only those services currently being rendered by the owner/applicant. Do not include future services.)

_____
_____
_____

2. (b) <u>TRADEMARK:</u> If the owner/applicant is using the name, logo, design and/or slogan being registered in connection with an actual product manufactured by the owner/applicant or on the owner/applicant's behalf, the mark is a trademark. If the mark is a trademark, the applicant/owner must list the specific product(s) the name, logo, design and/or slogan is being used to identify. For example: ladies sportswear, cat food, barbecue grills, shoe laces, etc. <u>If the owner/applicant is using the name, logo, design and/or slogan to identify goods available in the market place, enter the specific product(s) the name, logo, design and/or slogan is being used to identify:</u>

(Note: List only those product(s) currently available. Do not include future products.)

_____
_____
_____

2. (c) <u>HOW IS THE NAME, LOGO, DESIGN AND/OR SLOGAN CURRENTLY USED:</u>

<u>SERVICE MARKS:</u> If the name, logo, design and/or slogan are/is being used in connection with a type of service, you must specify the form(s)/mean(s) of advertisement the applicant/owner is using to advertise the services to the general public. For example: newspaper advertisements, business cards, brochures, flyers, pamphlets, menus, etc. <u>If the mark is being used in connection with a type of service, state how the name, logo, design and/or slogan are/is being used in advertising here:</u>

_____
_____
_____

<u>TRADEMARKS:</u> If the name, logo, design and/or slogan are/is being used to identify a product manufactured by or fore the applicant/owner, you must specify how the mark is applied or affixed to the actual product or its packaging. For example: a tag, label, imprinted or engraved on the actual product, etc. <u>If the mark is being used in connection with a specific product, state how the name, logo, design and/or slogan is applied or affixed to the actual product(s) or the packaging:</u>

_____
_____
_____

2. (d) <u>FEE(S) AND CLASS(ES):</u> There are a total of 45 classes or categories in which all products or services must be categorized. The fee to register a mark is $87.50 per class. Make check payable to Florida Department of State.

<u>List the class(es) which apply to the product(s) and/or service(s) listed in 2(a) and/or 2(b) above:</u>

_____
_____
_____

PART II

1. You must state the date the name, logo, design and/or slogan was first used in the state of Florida, and, if it was used in another state or country, the date you first used the name, logo, design and/or slogan in the other state or country. <u>Enter the month, day, and year the name, logo, design and/or slogan was first used by the applicant/owner, the predecessor, or a related company in Florida. If the name, logo, design and/or slogan has been used in another state or country, then you must also enter the month, day, and year the name, logo, design and/or slogan was/were used in another state or country, when applicable.</u>

Note: The Florida Statutes require a mark to be in use prior to registration.

(a) Date first used in other state or country, if applicable: _____

(b) Date first used in Florida: _____

PART III

ENTER NAME, LOGO, DESIGN AND/OR SLOGAN BEING REGISTERED:

1. Enter the name, a brief description of the logo or design, and/or the slogan you are registering. The description of the logo and/or design must be 25 words or less. List the exact name, slogan, and/or description of the logo/design here: (NOTE: The name, logo, design and/or slogan listed in this section must match the exact name, logo, design and/or slogan listed on your specimens or examples.)

_____

_____

_____

_____

Provide the English translation of any and all terms listed #1 above, when applicable:

_____

_____

2. DISCLAIMER STATEMENT (if applicable):

Your mark may include a word or design that is commonly used by others. Commonly used terms or designs must be disclaimed. When you disclaim a specific term or design, you are acknowledging this term is commonly used by others and that you do not claim the exclusive right to use the disclaimed term or design. All geographical terms and representations of cities, states or countries must be disclaimed (i.e., Miami, Orlando, Florida, the design of the state of Florida, the design of the United States of America, etc.). Corporate suffixes and terms readily associated with the specific product(s) and/or(s) service being provided must also be disclaimed.

<u>Enter all terms listed in #1 above which require a disclaimer in the space provided below:</u>

NO CLAIM IS MADE TO THE EXCLUSIVE RIGHT TO USE THE TERM(S)"

_____ "APART FROM THE MARK AS SHOWN.

3. ATTACH OR INCLUDE THREE SPECIMENS OR EXAMPLES OF THE TRADEMARK OR SERVICE MARK BEING REGISTERED

Chapter 495, F.S., requires you to submit three specimens (samples or examples) of the mark in use. You must submit three specimens FOR EACH CLASS listed in Part I #2(d). The name, logo, design and/or slogan on the specimens must be identical to the name, logo, design and/or slogan being registered. You may provide three identical specimens or three different specimens. For each service mark class (classes 35-45), you may provide three newspaper advertisements, business cards, brochures, flyers, or any combination thereof. For each trademark class (classes 1-34), you may provide three tags, labels, boxes, etc. or any combination thereof. Photographs of bulky specimens are acceptable if the mark being registered and the good(s) or product(s) are clearly legible.

SIGNATURE OF APPLICANT/OWNER AND NOTARIZATION:

I,_____, being sworn, depose and say that I am the owner and the applicant herein, or that I am authorized to sign on behalf of the owner and applicant herein, and to the best of my knowledge no other person except a related company has registered this mark in this state or has the right to use such mark in Florida either in the identical form thereof or in such near resemblance as to be likely, when applied to the goods or services of such other person to cause confusion, to cause mistake or to deceive. I make this affidavit and verification on my/the applicant's behalf. I farther acknowledge that I have read the application and know the contents thereof and that the facts stated herein are true and correct.

_____
Typed or printed name of applicant

_____
Applicant's signature
(List name and title)

STATE OF _____

COUNTY OF _____

Sworn to and subscribed before me on this_____day of_____,___.,
_____
(Name of Individual Signing)

☐ who is personally known to me   ☐ whose identity I proved on the basis of _____
_____

_____
Notary Public Signature

(Seal)
_____
Notary's Printed Name

My Commission Expires: _____

FILING FEE: $87.50 per class

Page 4 of 4

CHAPTER 3: PATENTS

PATENTS

All business with the patent and trademark office should be transacted in writing; and such attention will be based exclusively on the written record in the office.

As such, no attention will be paid to any alleged oral promise, stipulation, or understanding in relation to which there is disagreement or doubt.

Applicants and their attorneys and agents are required to conduct their business with the USPTO with decorum and courtesy. Papers presented in violation of this requirement will be submitted to the Director and will not be entered. A notice of the non-entering of the paper will be provided.

There is no minimum age for a person to be qualified to to execute an oath or declaration, but the person must be competent to execute, i.e., understand the document that the person is executing, and its contents within.

The Office provides forms to the public to use in certain situations to assist in the filing of correspondence for a certain purpose and to meet certain requirements for patent applications and proceedings. Use of the forms for purposes of which they were not designed is prohibited.

All specifications, drawings and papers related to a published application, patent, or statutory invention registration are open to inspection by the publics and copies may be obtained upon the payment of a fee, whether they be certified or non certified copies.

Only inventors or joint inventors can apply for patents; and each piece of correspondence requires a person's signature which may be an original handwriting signed in permanent dark ink.

Patent applications that have not been published are generally preserved in confidence.

Payments are made in U.S. dollars and in the form of a cashier's or certified check, treasury note, national bank note, or U.S. Postal Service money order. The office may cancel or delay the credit until full collection is made. Credit cards are not recommended due to the fact that the person's credit card no. may mistakenly end up as public knowledge.

Cheeks and money orders must be paid out to "Director of the United States Patent and Trademark Office," P.O. Box 1450, Alexandria, Virginia, 22313-1450

Correspondence received in the patent and trademark office is stamped with the date of receipt.

Except for correspondence received on Saturdays, Sundays and federal holidays, which will be stamped as received on the business day prior to Saturday, Sunday or the federal holiday.

Now of course I can sit here and go on and on about the general requisites of applying for a patent like (1) the specifications, (2) the inventor(s) oath or declaration, (3) necessary drawings, (4) the prescribed filing fee, search fee, examination fee, and application size fee, (5) a cover sheet identifying the name of the inventor(s), the residence of each named inventor, the title of invention, the name and register number of the attorney or agent, the document number used by the person filing the application, the corresponding address which mail is received and any other addresses if different from where said mail is received, (6) the mandated requirements of the paper being flexible, strong, smooth, non shiny, durable, and written in an plainly and legibly form by either a typewriter or machine printer in permanent dark ink; and only on one side in portrait orientation, And (7) that the page be 1½ or double spaced, and preferably in a font size of 12.

However, I feel like this book is your teacher and as a teacher I want to give you the most soundest instruction: That this is an extremely comprehensive and complicated field that MUST be guided through or carried out by the guiding hand of an patent attorney. The laws and expertise in this field is non short of mandating professional representation.

OVERVIEW

Overall, always remember the difference between the three: Copyright, Trademark/Service Mark, and Patent.

a. Copyright offers a form of written or expressed protection;

b. Trademark/Service Mark offers a form of designer image protection;

c. And Patent offers a protection based on the form and operation of a design.

I've had many people confuse the three so make sure you know what you're talking about when faced with someone whom doesn't.

DOMAIN NAMES

DOMAIN NAMES

A domain name is a internet address assigned by "Icann" (Internet Corporation for Assigned Names and Numbers). Those addresses are procured, and sometimes secured, by internet service providers, whom then in turn, resale, rent, or lease the addresses to another party.

Those internet service providers are companies like Google, Yahoo, Go Daddy, 1and1 and etc.

These domain name providers are in competition with eachother and they all add competitive features with the purchasing of a domain name from their company.

Majority of those features consists of a specific amount of internet space to build your website, in addition to company hosting, wherein the domain name provider runs and operates your website for an affordable monthly fee.

Whichever domain name provider you choose to procure your domain name from, you are making one of the best investments you could ever imagine by doing so for your company, business or project.

The history on domain names is that some people chose occupations to simply sit at home all day and conjure thoughts of creative domain names, and thus sold them for multi-million dollars when companies came calling for them because said name fitted their business services better than the one they came up with on their own.

Imagine if you had the domain name "www.nike.com," well Nike would have bargained with you for millions of dollars for that internet address. So whenever you arrive with the idea of your business name or business concept, then purchase your domain name for it as soon as you can. If its taken then someone else already has it and or are already doing or thinking similar to what you have thought of or are doing. And if that be the case then be creative and come up with something else. But most importantly, obtain the domain name before someone else does. Because the old saying is true, that nothing new is thought of under the sun. Timing is the only factor that matter.

There's something else important you need to know. Don't just submit your domain name to a service provider just to see if its available. If you do that then....you're *#@%ed. What your internet service provider does is sends the domain name listing to "Icann" and register it for themselves. Then, when you actually are ready to purchase and secure the domain name for yourself, the domain name will then be unavailable, and now offered for sale at a price more expensive than it was when you initially sought its availability; and for much more than the average domain name fee.

When selecting your distinct domain name(s), you should be aware that the domain name's availability depends on the faet of rather the domain name is already purchased or not. If the domain name is unavailable, then that specific domain name can't be purchased and another one have to be selected. The best way to determine whether a domain name is available, without entering it into any internet service provider system, is to visit www.whois.com. Said website allows you to scroll its database of domain names, in its alphabetical order, without entering the domain name into the computer. If the domain name doesn't appear then its highly likely that the domain name is available for you to purchase.

Visiting the "whois.com" website allows you to view a wide database of domain names that Grants you the insight of selecting a creative, distinct domain name for your company, business or project. You will notice that some domain name owners purchase groups of domain names surrounding the domain name they choose, for protection of securing every domain name that could sound similar to theirs. For example: a person might secure www.XXX.com. He may also secure www.xxxrated.com, www.ratedx.com, www.ratedxxx.com etc. In this regard, he secures all domain names that could be confused with his, in the event he builds the XXX brand up to global recognition. By this, no one could confuse his brand with another and spend money with the similar brand because of the mistake.

Now since I mentioned that, I want to inform you on this method called "Cyber Squatting."

Cyber Squatting is similar to what I just mentioned, only the intent is willful. It consists of the registration, use, or trafficking in a domain name that is identical or confusingly similar to a distinctive or famous domain name or trademark, with a bad intent to profit from such use. Higher authorities then recognized domain names as INTERNET REALESTATE and created a law to prohibit such violations called "The AntiCybersquatting Consumer Protection Act" (the ACPA).

To determine whether a person possesses the required bad-faith intent to profit from the domain name, courts considers nine factors:

(1) the trademark or other intellectual property rights of the domain name owner, if any, within the domain name, (2) the extent to which the domain names consist of the legal name or commonly used names of the domain name owner, (3) the domain name owner's prior use of the domain name(s) for the bona fide offering of goods or services, (4) any bona fide noncommercial or fair use of the mark under the domain names, (5) the perpetrator's intent to divert consumers from the domain name owner's website by creating a likelihood of confusion, (6) the perpetrator's offer to transfer, sell, or otherwise assign the domain names to the perpetrator or others for financial gain, (7) the perpetrator's provision of material and misleading false contact information when registering the domain names and its intentional failure to maintain accurate contact information, (8) the perpetrator's registration or acquisition of multiple domain names that they know are identical or confusingly similar to marks or domain names of others, and

(9) the extent to which the perpetrator marks or domain names are or are not distinctive and famous. 15 U.S.C. §§1125(d)(l)(B)(i)(I) -- (IX).

Statutory damages for Cyber Squatting range from "not less than $1,000 dollars and not more than $100,000 dollar per domain name," as the court considers gust, 15 U.S.C. §1117(d). The maximum amount is $2,000,000 dollars in statutory damages under the Lanham Act when the court finds that the intent was willful.

ONCE DOMAIN NAME IS PROCURED

Once your domain name is procured, create a website using the amount of web space provided by your domain name service provider. Even if its just to let visitors know that the website is in its early stages of web building and or operations.

SECURITY BADGE

When creating the website be sure to implement a "payment Processor" program that accepts online payments by credit credit cards.

A important factor that you want to focus on is incorporating a "Security Badge" on its home page, wherein visitors can clearly see, that informs them that their private and personal information is safe, secure and encrypted; and that such information is not shared and or sold with third parties.

HOW TO OBTAIN A DOMAIN NAME

To purchase and obtain a domain name is procured by the following steps:
a. Pick up a prepaid debit card (preferably a visa that have never been used) and load it with approximately $50 dollars;
b. Visit an online domain name service provider such as Google, Yahoo, Go Daddy and or landl.

In my opinionated research www.landl.com is by far the best domain name provider in the game. Their services and domain name packages are unmatched. In addition, their fees for their domain name services are also unmatched, and a domain name from their company costs only $8.99 a year and you own the domain name as long as you pay the annual $8.99 fee. No other company comes close to the package and domain name fees offered by them;

c. Once you visit your domain name service provider, you will then follow their given instructions and enter your domain name with all of its characters (for example: www.turntupentertainment.com). If the name is not available then you will have to choose another one. If the domain name is available then follow their instructions and provide them with your credit card information, paying for the domain names;

d. Move to build a small website with a clean aesthetic look, with the available amount of domain name space given with your domain name(s);

e. Move then to add a "payment processor" that accepts online payments;

f. And finally, add a badge on the home page of the website wherein visitors will clearly notice that their private and personal information are safe, secure and encrypted and not shared and or sold to third parties.

Simply having the domain name and website is essential and will give your website a professional business look, even when the business is not yet operating. **[I'll show you later how it is so relevant.]**

CHAPTER 5
CORPORATIONS

CORPORATIONS

Now we're getting to the essential parts: Corporations. Corporations are business entities that Govern most of America's employment. To own one is a great privilege to exercise. And to maximize the benefits of one, takes insider knowledge and creative thinking. This is where this book comes into play.

However, before you do anything, find your state and send a letter requesting either a registration form for a L.L.C. or either a registration form for a "C" corporation (for profit). You also need to inquire of their fees to file both entities and the mandated requirements that Govern such entities. Below is a list of states within the U.S. Find your state and request the stated documents:

Alabama

Corporations Division
Office of the Secretary of State
P.O. Box 5616
Montgomery, Alabama 36103-5616
or visit http://www.sos.state.al.us/business/corporations.cfm

Alaska

The Division of Banking, Securities and Corporations
Department of Community and Economic Development
P.O. Box 110808
Juneau, Ak 99801-0808
or visit http://www.dced.state.ak.us/bsc/corpdoc.htm

Arizona

Arizona Corporation Commission
Corporations Division
1300 West Washington
Phoenix, Az. 85007-2996
or visit http://www.cc.state.az.us

Arkansas

Secretary of State
256 State Capital Building
Little Rock, Ar. 72201
or visit http://www.sosweb.state.ar.us/

California

Business Program Division
1500 11th Street
Sacramento, Ca. 95814
or visit http://www.ss.ca.gov/business/corp/corporate.htm

Colorado

Department of State
Business Services
1560 Broadway, Suite 200
Denver, Co. 80202
or visit http://www.sos.state.co.us/pubs/business/main.htm

Connecticut

Secretary of State's Office
210 Capital Avenue, Suite 104
Hartford, CT. 06106
or visit http://www.sots.state.ct.us/

Delaware
State of Delaware
Division of Corporations
401 Federal Street, Suite 4
Dover, Delaware 19901
or visit http://www.state.de.us/corp/index.htm

Florida
Division of Corporations
P.O. Box 6327
Tallahassee, FL. 32314
or visit http://www.dos.state.fl.us/index.html

Georgia
Corporations Division
315 West Tower
2 Martin Luther King, Jr. Drive
Atlanta, GA. 30334
or visit http://www.sos.state.ga.us/corporations/

Hawaii
Department of Commerce and Consumer Affairs
Business Registration Division
P.O. Box 40
Honolulu, Hawaii 96810
or visit http://www.businessregistrations.com/index.html

Idaho
Office of the Secretary of State
700 W. Jefferson, Room 203
P.O. Box 83720
Boise, ID. 83720-0080
or visit http://www.idsos.state.id.us/

Illinois

Secretary of State
Department of Business Services
Springfield, Il. 62756
or visit http://www.sos.state.il.us

Indiana

Indiana Secretary of State
Business Services
302 W. Washington
Room E-018
Indianapolis, IN. 46204
or visit http://www.ai.org/sos/bus_service/

Iowa

Business Services Division
Office of the Secretary of State
1305 E. Walnut
2nd Floor Hoover Bldg.
Des Moines, Iowa 50319
or visit http://www.sos.state.ia.us/business/services.html

Kansas

Kansas Secretary of State
Corporations Division
120 SW 10th Ave., Room 100
Topeka, KS. 66612-1240
or visit http://www.kssos.org/corpwelc.html

Kentucky

Kentucky Secretary of State
700 Capital Ave.
Suite 152, State Capital
Frankfort, KY. 40601
or visit http://www.sos.state.ky.us/

Louisiana

Louisiana Secretary of State
Commercial Division
P.O. Box 94125
Baton Rouge, LA. 70804
or visit http://www.sec.state.la.us/comm-index.htm

Maine

Maine Department of the Secretary of State Bureau of Corp.
Elections and Commissions
101 State House Station
Augusta, ME. 04333-0101
or visit http://www.state.me.us/sos/cec/corp/corp.htm

Maryland

Corporate Records
301 W. Preston Street
Room 801
Baltimore, Maryland 21201-2395
or visit http://www.dat.state.md.us/sdatweb/charter.html

Massachusetts

The Corporations: Divisions of the Secretary of the Commonwealth's Office
One Ashbuvton Place
Boston, MA. 02108-1512
or visit http://www.state.ma.us/see/cor/coridx.htm

Michigan

Bureau of Commercial Services
Corporation Division
P.O. Box 30054
Lansing, MI. 48909
or visit http://www.cis.state.mi.us/corp/

Minnesota

Business Services Director
Minnesota Secretary of State
180 State Office Building
100 Constitution Avenue
Saint Paul, MN. 55155-1299
or visit http://www.sos.state.mn.us/business/index.html

Mississippi

Business Services division
Mississippi Secretary of State
P.O. Box 136
Jackson, MS. 39205
or visit www.sos.state.ms.us/busserv/corp/corporations.html

Missouri

Corporations Division
James C. Kirkpatrick State Information Center
P.O. Box 7:78
Jefferson City, Missouri 65102
or visit http://mosl.sos.state.mo.us/bus-ser/soscor.html

Montana

Business Service Bureau
Secretary of State
State Capital, Room 260
P.O. Box 202801
Helena, Montana 59620-2801
or visit http://state.mt.us/sos/index.htm

Nebraska

Nebraska Secretary of State, Corporate Division
State Capital, Room 1301
Lincoln, Nebraska 68509
or visit http://www.nol.org/business.html

Nevada

Corporate Recordings/Corporate Information
Secretary of State-Annex Office
202 N. Carson Street
Carson City, Nevada 89701-4271
or visit http://sos.state.nv.us/

New Hampshire

New Hampshire Secretary of State
Corporate division
25 Capital Street, Floor 3
Concord, NH. 03301-6312

New Jersey

Division of Revenue
P.O. Box 308
Trenton, NJ. 08625
or visit http://www.state.nj.us/treasury/revenue/dcr/dcrpgl.html

New Mexico

State Corporation Commission
Corporation Department
P.O. Box 1269
Sante Fe, New Mexico 87504-1269
(505) 827-4511 (call for web address)

New York

New York State Department of State
Division of Corporations, State Records and
Uniform Commercial Code
41 State Street
Albany, NY. 12231-0001
or visit http://www.dos.state.ny/corp/corp.html

North Carolina
Corporation of Division
P.O. Box 29622
Raleigh, NC. 27626-0622
or visit http://www.secretary.state.nc.us/corporations/

North Dakota
Secretary of State
600 E. Boulevard Ave., Dept. 108
Bismark, ND 58505-0500
or visit www.sosbir@state.nd.us

Ohio
Ohio Secretary of State
180 E. Broad Street, 16th Floor
Columbus, Ohio 43215
or visit http://www.state.oh.us/sos/

Oklahoma
Janet Sullivan, Director
Corporations Division
Public Service Building
255 Capital St., NE, Suite 151
Salem, OR 97310-1327
or visit http://www.sos.state.or.us/corporation/bic/bic.htm

Pennsylvania
Department of State
Corporation Bureau
P.O. Box 8722
Harrisburg, PA. 17105-8722
or visit http://www.dos.state.pa.us/corp/index.htm

Rhode Island

First Stop Business Center
100 Worth Main, Street, 2nd Floor
Providence, RI. 02903-1335
or visit http://www.sec.state.ri.us/bus/frststp.htm

South Carolina

South Carolina Secretary of State
Business Filings
P.O. Box 11350
Columbia, SC. 29211
or visit http://www.sasos.com/

South Dakota

Secretary of State
Capital Building
500 East Capital Avenue, Suite 204
Pierre, SD 57501-5070
or visit http://www.state.sd.us/sos/sos.htm

Tennessee

Division of Business Services
312 Eighth Avenue, North
6th Floor, William R. Snodgrass Tower
Nashville, TN 37243
or visit http://www.state.tn.us/sos/service.htm

Texas

Corporations Section
Secretary of State
P.O. Box 13697
Austin, TX. 78711
or visit http://www.sos.state.tx.us/corp/index.shtml

Utah

Utah department of Commerce
Division of Corporation and Commercial Code
160 E. 300th Street
Salt Lake City, UT. 84111
or visit http://www.commerce.state.ut.us/corporat/corpcoc.htm

Vermont

Vermont Secretary of State
Corporation Division
81 River Street, Drawer 09
Montpelier, VT. 05609-1104
or visit http://www.sec.state.vt.us/corps/corpindex.htm

Virginia

Office of the Clerk
Virginia State Corporation Division
P.O. Box 1197
Richmond, Virginia 23218
or visit http://www.state.va.us/scc/division/clk/index.htm

Washington

Corporations Division
801 Capital Way, South
Olympia, WA. 98504-0234
or visit http://www.secstate.wa.gov/corps/default.htm

West Virginia

Corporations Divisions
Secretary of State
Bldg. 1, Suite 157-K
1900 Kanawha Blvd., East
Charleston, WV. 25305-0770
or visit http://www.state.wv.us/sos/corp/default.htm

Wisconsin

Corporations Section, 3rd Floor
P.O. Box 7846
Madison, WI. 53707-7846
or visit www.wdfi.org/corporations/

Wyoming

Secretary of State
Corporations Division
200 West 24th Street
The Capital Building
Cheyenne 82002-0020
or visit http://soswy.state.wy.us/corporat/corporat.htm

Now that I've covered this area lets move on.

This is an enlightening section about secrets and strategies that the rich have used for years, to run their corporations, protect their assets, secure funding and save huge money in taxes. By the time you finish this book you should be equipped with the necessary knowledge and creative entrepreneur skills to make fortunes from your corporation. And although I don't provide all the advantages and disadvantages of running a corporation, the strategies and secrets that I do teach are ones that will reap you lucrative rewards if lawfully applied. Now shall we begin.

CONVICTED FELONS

Once upon a time convicted felons were frowned upon in society as disfunctional citizens. Today, that outlook does not hold the same unless such individuals honestly fits the bill.

With more than 2.3 million U.S. citizens incarcerated, a number more than some countries populations, the law seems to depict that our justice symbols really resembles what it portrays: a blindfolded, uneven statute.

Convicted felons however, without ever knowing better, all commonly thought that such a strike on their record have prohibited them from owning certain licenses. For example, If I was a convicted felon, then how could I own a gun shop? Or how could I own a liquor license? **Pay very close attention here because this game alone is worth the title of the book.**

The answer to both of these questions are simple: I have someone incorporate and I own the corporation through being a majority share holder (that's right, the chairman).

And the most wonderful thing about it is that its perfectly legal.

I can own anything the law says that I can't have, as long as I don't own it in my personal capacity. It only becomes 'illegal' when I go about securing these things in my personal capacity. Say I'm a convicted felon and I want a bail bond company. No problem, I just incorporate.

But what I'm here to teach you is that most corporations that you'll choose, will not be companies that you will have to walk a chalk line in. So for starters **stay away from** any companies that deal with **alcohol, tobacco and firearms.** The companies that you want to more likely be choosing is companies in fields unrelated to the ones I just mentioned. I'm not discounting that you can't own a alcohol, tobacco and or firearm corporation, but if you choose to, the line you must walk must be so thin that you have to basically have no hands-on involvement with its operations, other than bookkeeping. Now that we got this clarified, lets move on.

TYPES OF CORPORATIONS

There are seven types of corporations, they are:
1. Sole Proprietorship
2. General Partnership
3. Limited Partnership
4. Limited Liability Partnership
5. S Corporation
6. LLC (Limited Liability Company)

7. C Corporation

Each of them have their own advantages and disadvantages. And each of them must be chosen independently for your own unique and specific purpose. To make it much clear on the point, one size does not fit all. However, I'm not going to waste your time with what each of them could do. If you're that interested and serious concerning that matter then you will purchase you a book on the subjects of "corporations and how they're maximized." (this is not a specific book title)

My main concern here is to show you what the ones will do that I'm familiar with and know about. Those that I intend to speak of are surefire money machines; and the rest of them doesn't provide near the protection, security, tax benefits and funding capabilities that they offer. These corporations are called the LLC and the C corporation.

We will describe the LLC as the People's Choice because of its capabilities. We will describe the C corporation as the MVP of corporations because of its capabilities. But before we get into either of these two entities, lets talk about the simplicity of establishing them:

SIMPLICITY OF CORP. ESTABLISHING

Forming a corporation is somewhat simple. You file a document that creates an independent legal entity with a life of its own. It has its own name, business purpose and tax identity with the IRS. As such, the corporation is responsible for the activities of the business. In this way the owners, shareholders or members are protected. The owner's liability is limited to the monies they used to start the corporation, and not any of their personal assets. **A quick reminder, your corporation's name shall be the exact same as your domain name.**

If an entity is to be sued, it is the corporation and not the individuals behind the legal entity.

The corporation is organized by one or more shareholders or members. Depending upon each state's law, it may allow one person to serve as all officers and directors, or the sole member.

In certain states nominee officers, directors or members may be utilized to protect the owner's privacy.

A corporation's first filing, "The Articles of Incorporation" is signed by the incorporator, which in most states, is someone over the age of 18 years old. The incorporator may be an individual that's not even involved in the company.

The articles of incorporation set out the company's name, the initial board of directors, the authorised number of shares and or the members and managers of the corporation and each of the members or managers interest in the company. The corporation is then Governed by its Bylaws and its decisions are subsequently recorded in the corporation's "Meeting Minutes," which are kept in the corporate minute book.

When the corporation is issued its "Certificate of Status" the company must then be handed over from the incorporator, which is someone whom merely register's the company with the Secretary of State. The shareholders and or members then appoint Directors or General Managers to carry out the day to day management and affairs of the company.

The Directors, and or Managers must remember to follow corporate formalities. They must treat the corporation as a separate and independent legal entity, which includes holding regular scheduled meetings, conduct banking through a separate corporate bank account, file separate corporate tax returns, and file other corporate documents with the state on a timely basis.

Failure to follow such formalities may allow a creditor to disregard the corporate veil and seek personal liability against the corporate officers, directors, General Managers, etc., in their individual capacities. This is known as "Piercing the corporate veil," a legal maneuver in which creditors attempts to establish that the corporation failed to operate as a separate distinct entity. If this happens then the veil of corporate protection is pierced and the individuals involved are held personal liable for any debts, claims or damages of the corporation.

So, adhering to corporate formalities are not at all difficult or particularly time consuming.

THE DIFFERENCE BETWEEN LLC & C CORPORATIONS

Now lets talk about the difference between LLCs and C Corporations, regarding each of their advantages, starting first with the LLC.

a. The LLC can be managed by one member;
b. Could be managed by a non-member;
c. Could be managed by a manager;
d. Has flow through taxation (instead of being taxed at the corporate and individual level);
e. Has flexible management structure;
f. Has flexible allocation of profit and losses;
g. Has liability protection;
h. Could have one or unlimited members;
i. Its members or managers could be foreign citizens, spendthrifts, Trusts, other corporations, etc.;
j. Its membership interest have no restrictions of prohibited membership purchasers;
k. It could have several layers of management supervision;
l. It allows beneficial restrictions on transfers;
m. It can carry on with a unanimous vote of members after the death of a majority interest holder;
n. It can receive benefits associated with C corporations;
o. And it has buy-back provisions or rights of first refusal.

Now here's some of the advantages of C corporations:
a. It can have just one shareholder;
b. It has the option of hiring a Board of Directors;
c. Business expenses are not treated as income to shareholders;
d. It has no personal liability to shareholders;

e. The corporation continues after the death of a majority shareholder;
f. It can deduct for the future expansion of the business;
g. It has the ability to issue 1244 stock;
h. Can have unlimited shareholders;
i. Can be owned by a trust or another corporation;
j. Can be owned by a foreigner;
k. Its freely transferable, absent restrictions on shareholder agreements;
l. Can issue founder's shares;
m. Founders can purchase shares at 0.001 (one tenth of one cent per share);
n. Can have private placements;
o. Can go public;
p. Can offer medicare, group life, dental and disability insurance. And additionally allow reimbursement of employee medical; travel, ground and other expenses;
q. and other privileges.

The C corporation can also deduct the following expenses as being associated with overhead and or business expenses:

a. Office rent;
b. Start-up expenses;
c. Meals;
d. Office Equipment;
e. Telephone expenses;
f. Employee expenses;
g. Vehicle leases;
h. Achievement awards;
i. Travel expenses;
j. Dependent care;
k. Cafeteria plan;
l. Educational expenses;
m. Retirement plans;
n. Lower tax rate;
o. Saleries;
p. Pension plans;
q. Passive activity losses;
r. Entertainment;

s. Homes, vehicles, boats, airplanes, etc.;
t. Accounting fees;
u. Advertising;
v. Amortization;
w. Bad debts that the corporation cannot collect;
x. Banking fees;
y. Board meetings; travels, stays, and transportation associated with it;
z. Corporation property repairs and maintenance;
z1. Business association membership dues;
z2. Charity deductions;
z3. Cleaning services;
z4. Collection expenses;
z5. Commissions to outside parties;
z6. Consulting fees;
z7. Conventions and tradeshows;
z8. Seminars;
z9. Costs of goods sold;
z10. Credit card convenience fees;
z11. Depreciations;
z12. Discounts to customers;
z13. Equipment repairs;
z14. Exhibits for publicity;
z15. Marketing and promotions;
z16. Franchise fees;
z17. Freight and shipping costs;
z18. Furniture and or fixtures;
z19. Interest;
z20. Internet hosting and services;
z21. Investment advice and fees;
z22. Legal fees;
z23. License fees;
z24. License due to theft;
z25. Management fees;
z26. Materials;
z27. Newspapers and magazines;
z28. Outside services;

z29. Parking and Tolls;
z30. Postage;
z31. Research and Development;
z32. Royalties;
z33. Safety Deposit Box;
z34. Safe;
z35. Software and online services;
z36. Storage rental;
z37. Subcontractors;
z38. Taxes;
z39. Security;
z40. Utilities;
z41. Web design;

and whatever else you think that you can think of and tie to being a business expense.

As you can see why the C corporation is the MVP of corporations. However, the LLC offers its own unique benefits as well. One is just on a smaller scale with the expectations to grow to a larger one (LLC) and the other is already on a larger scale with the expectations to stay large (C corp.). Just remember what I said earlier: one size does not fit all, and you have to choose the one that works best for what you're looking for, and where you wanna take yourself. The most important thing to know is that these two corporations Grants you the best of whatever world you choose to reside in. In this day and age wherein litigation can unexpectedly wipe out a lifetime of savings, FULL and limited liability protections are of paramount importance.

DIRECTORS

Allow me to familiarise you with the definition of "Director" or "Board of Director."

Directors or Board of Directors are people whom you appoint to run your company (if you chose the C corporation). They're (in order) CEO (chief executive officers), Executive Secretary(s), Treasurers, Presidents, Vice

Presidents, CFO (chief finance officers), COO (chief operating officers), CSO (chief security officers), etc. get my drift?

If the corporation belonged to you, as the majority share holder and founder, then your position will be held to its highest amongst the Board. That position is The Chairman. If one strictly understood the structure of a corporation, then he or she would ultimately see the bigger picture of Presidents (even presidents of countries). They're button pushers, puppets and fall guys that is directed to carry out the command of the Board, which makes up a chairman and the rest of the committee. If you've ever watched politic at work you will clearly see this point of view, knowing well aware that America is a big corporation whom has a president to oversee its affairs.

However, the Board of Directors within a corporation holds an enormous amount of power and control over the actions of the business. They are responsible for the direction and positive operations of the company. They can call meetings among themselves, sign contracts binding the company to various obligations, conduct purchases and sales of various assets; and incur debt in the company's name.

They can appoint and terminate at any time by a majority of a vote; regulate the sale and transfer of the company shares, including the price for purchases and sales, and control the company's bank account, including who may or may not sign checks.

There's no way possible that potential investors will invest in your corporation without clean, responsible officers, members or managers.

With the type of power that will be vested in them, investors will want to know that their investments are safe and Governed in good faith, with reasonable belief that the company's best interest is acknowledged first.

Now as it regards an LLC, there is no Board of Directors, only what is called "Member Managed and Manager Managed." A Member Manager is someone whom is also a shareholder in the LLC. I used shareholder to get your attention. There is actually no such thing as a shareholder in a LLC. It is Governed by percent ownership. For instance, someone whom has a 50% interest in the company (LLC). So the 'member manager will be a person holding a interest.

The 'managing manager' is someone whom is simply managing the LLC on behalf of others. In essence, he is the Board of Directors in the sense of if the LLC was a C corporation. However, the managing member has no interest whatsoever in the LLC, he simply manage the LLC affairs and report back to the Interest owners.

I hope I provided you with enough insight on these topics without making it seem complicated or hard to grasp, Its really not.

EMPLOYEE ISSUES

Allow me now to fill you in on "employee issues." You must determine four things when it comes to this particular area:

1. Should you hire employees or independent contractors;
2. The ins and outs of the Employee Agreement;
3. The basics of employment laws;
4. and the basics of employee benefits.

Lets begin first with 'should you hire employees or independent contractors.'

EMPLOYEES OR INDEPENDENT CONTRACTORS

When deciding should you hire employees or independent contractors, you have to think about things like payroll, state and federal taxes, workers compensations, health care plans and benefits, pension and other benefits, salary and performance reviews, paid holidays and overtime, sick time, severance pay, etc. **Be mindful that if you're the sole shareholder or managing member, then you won't have any employee issues with the IRS regarding this matter.**
Otherwise, you can bring someone in to handle your work for you and pay them for it. This person is called an Independent Contractor. They assume all responsibility for all of the expenses stated above. So the company is otherwise exempt from any liabilities associated with traditional employer/employee relationships.

So an Independent Contractor may be your best bet when it comes to employee issues. All that is required is that you enter into a Independent Contractor Service Agreement. But be careful because the IRS have a certain criteria they follow in determining the difference between the two.

Now, lets move forward to the ins and outs of the Employee Agreement:

EMPLOYEE AGREEMENT

Employee agreements, as with independent contractor service agreements, are essential to attracting venture capital and other funding. But this is just a tip of the benefits held. Such agreements protects employees from selling the company's valuable information and operating secrets to competitors; or better yet, prohibit the employee from breaking away from the company and going into business competing with the company head on. And there's many more conjuring protections like spelling out responsibilities, scope of duties, terms of the agreement, hours of employment, termination clauses, etc.

Now lets visit the basics of employee laws.

EMPLOYEE LAWS

There are certain federal laws dealing with employment issues that must be strictly abided by. Laws like minimum wage, equal pay, overtime, child labor, The Fair Labor Standards Act (FLSA), The Civil Rights Act of 1964 (CRA), The age Discrimination and Employment ACt (ADEA), The American Disabilities Act (ADA), The Occupational Safety and Health Act (OSHA), Workers Compensation, The Employment Polygraph Protection Act (EPPA), The Electronic Communications Privacy Act of 1986 (ECPA), etc.

Though there are a great many independent services that will accept the job of overseeing this department in your corporation, you must still familiarize yourself with the knowledge and language of them, if your plan is to hire employees instead of independent contractors.

Now lets go over the final point: the basics of employee benefits.

EMPLOYEE BENEFITS

There are other regulations that you must familiarize yourself with as well, should employees become your main focus of company operations.

These regulations are Governed by 'employee benefits' and such benefits consists of: The Family and Medical Leave Act (FMLA), Employee Benefit Plans, Traditional Benefits, Tax-Qualified Retirement Plans, Section 401(k) Plan, Supplemental Compensation Benefits, Equity-Based Benefits, Stock Purchase Plans, Incentive Stock Option Plan, Phantom Stock and Stock Appreciation Rights, etc.

As I stated earlier, be sure that you understand what these laws and regulations are about when and if you intend to hire employees, instead of Independent Contractors.

Now lets take a look at how **HARD** it is for the corporate veil to be pierced. I use the term HARD because if one can't remember abiding by something so simple, then they're going to have quite a problem being responsible.

All that is necessary for the corporate veil **NOT** to be pierced is that you:
a. Secure your 'EIN' number from the IRS after you receive your "Certified Certificate of Status" from your Secretary of State;
b. That you conduct all of your operations under a 'Corporate Notice,' meaning that you attach the suffix of "L.L.C.," "INC.," "CORP.," "COMPANY," or "CO." at the end of your business name, **On every piece of** document that exist regarding your business;
c. That you keep separate business accounts regarding your corporation;
d. That you hold annual meetings and keep records of those meetings in a place that they could be retrieved at sudden notice;
e. And that you submit annual filings to your Secretary of State, **along with the appropriate fees,** of those records, in a timely manner, that is set by Your Secretary of State's office.

With this accomplished, the corporate veil can **never** be pierced. Remember, its important to purchase a book in the field title of "how to run your own corporation." These books provides more in-dept knowledge of running a corporation. It also provides other valuable insights such as other limited liability protections, unlimited ownerships, flexible managements, distribution of profits, loses and special allocations, flow-through taxations, restrictions on transfers, family wealth transfers, sale or exchange of stock, unique corporate structuring, common voting shares, nonvoting shares, by laws, charging orders, corporate formalities, operating agreements, employee issues, health insurance and retirement plans, buy-sell agreements, personal holding companies and more.

HOW TO INCORPORATE

I need you to pay close attention on "How to Incorporate." Here, I'll provide you with insight on how to incorporate with both a C corporation and an LLC.
We'll start with the C corporation first.

COVER LETTER of a C CORPORATION

There should always be a cover letter to your incorporated documents, whether you're incorporating a C corporation or a LLC. Such cover should contain certain information of the Incorporator, a person whom I highly recommend as having a clean record. Their personal information should consist of things like: their name, city, address, zip code, daytime phone number, email address, etc. All information on the cover page shall be:

a. **SUBJECT:** The subject means that you must list the name of your corporation, along with the end suffix of Inc., Corporation, Corp., Company, or Co.;
b. Next you will check the box that requests: The filing fee, certified copy and certificate of status. You wanna purchase each of those features;
c. Next you want to list the full name, address, city, state, zip code and day time phone number of the Incorporator.
d. As it regards the email, I recommend providing the email of your, domain name.

This will conclude the cover page for your C corporation.

Next page is its "Articles of Incorporation." This must be a detailed document that cannot be left out of filing with your Secretary of State.

a. ARTICLE I, This should be the name of your incorporation exactly as its spelled on your cover page;
b. ARTICLE II, This must be the **Principal** office address of the corporation (This address could also be a home address);
c. ARTICLE III, This, is the corporation's purpose of operations. For example: Operating in the field of _____ and all other operations within such realm within state and federal laws;
d. ARTICLE IV, This is the corporation's authorised Shares section, which shall state: 100,000 non voting shares; and or any other number of shares fixed by the Board of Directors, whom are authorized within the limits and restrictions stated therein the Resolutions;
e. ARTICLE V, This is the corporation's initial Officers and Directors. That is, the corporation's CEO, Executive Secretary, Treasurer, President, Vice president, etc.

In most states, you can be the sole Board of Directors. That means that you can act as a Chairman until and if you decide to appoint other Officers;

f. ARTICLE VI, This is the corporation's Registered Agent, someone whom accepts mail on behalf of the corporation that is independent of the corporation. For this position I recommend it be your Incorporator. However, it can be you;
g. ARTICLE VII, This Article asks you to list your Incorporator, which is the same person listed on your cover page.

When all of this is completed, the Registered Agent and the Incorporator must sign and date the application. I recommend that the application be notarised before mailing it to the Secretary of State with the appropriate U.S. Postal Money Order. Payments however, can also be paid by credit card.

Now lets move on to the LLC.

The beginning of an LLC Registration starts first with the "COVER PAGE."

Beginning is the 'SUBJECT' which should be the name of your LLC.

The name of the LLC should end with the words "Limited Liability Company," either L.L.C., LLC; and the word limited could be abbrieviated as "Ltd." and the word company may be abbrieviated as "Co."

Followed is the Name of your Incorporator; The name of your company again; address; city, state and zip code; and email address. As with the C corporation, I recommend the email address of your company's domain name.

You must subsequently list the name of a person whom can be contacted regarding the LLC filing, along with their area code and a daytime phone number that they can be reached at.

Finally, you must choose the selective box that requests the filing fee, Certificate of Status and a Certified Copy of all. Its more than worth it to pay for the entire ordeal, in order for your company to appear professional.

Now we'll move on to the Articles of Organization. In most states the name of a Limited Liabilty company must be distinguishable and in some cases, you can conduct a preliminary name search with your Secretary of State prior to registering your company. This prevents trademark, service mark and copyright infringements.

ARTICLE I, should be the name of your LLC, exactly as it is spelled on the 'cover sheet,' and don't forget about the suffixes that must be attached to the end of the company's name;

ARTICLE II, should be the mailing and street address regarding the **Principal** office of the company;

ARTICLE III, should be the name, address (P.O. Box **NOT** accepted), City, State and Zip Code of your **Registered Agent.** The Registered Agent's signature is also required. Note: I recommend your Registered Agent be the same as your Incorporator listed on the Cover page of the Registration form.

ARTICLE IV, should be the name, address, City, State and Zip Code of your Member Manager or Managing Manager. You must list "MGR" for for every manager and "MGRM" for each managing member.

Don't forget! the member manager is the person in which holds ownership in the company. The managing manager is just a person that is managing the company independent of its owners.

ARTICLE V, List the specific date of filing. I recommend waiting on the file date of the Secretary of State's stamp and then allow that date to be the effective date of filing. However, this requirement is optional and if you do decide to list an effective date, list the date you initially began operations, but the date listed must be specific and cannot be more than five business days prior to the filing or 90 days after the date of filing.

A member of the company's signature is required thereafter.

Along with a printed name using non cursive writing.

Notorizing the LLC application is also recommended.

This concludes the filing of both the C corporation and the LLC; and prior to filing you must submit the original and one copy of whatever application you choose to register.

Note: There's two differences between the filings of the LLC and the C corporation.

The C corporation has a Article of Incorporation, while the LLC has the Article of Organization.

On the next page is an LLC form; a 'C' Corporation form and a bank resolution paper that you will need to duplicate and use to incorporate and open your corporate checkings and savings account, should you choose to do things yourself.

FLORIDA DEPARTMENT OF STATE
DIVISION OF CORPORATIONS

Attached are the forms and instructions to form a Florida Limited Liability Company pursuant to Chapter 608, Florida Statutes. All information included in the Articles of Organization must be in English and must be typewritten or printed legibly. If this requirement is not met, the document will be returned for correction(s). The Division of Corporations suggests using the sample articles merely as a guideline. Pursuant to s. 608.407, Florida Statutes, additional information may be contained in the Articles of Organization.

The name of a limited liability company must be distinguishable on the records of the Florida Department of State.

A preliminary search for name availability can be made on the Internet through the Division's records at www.sunbiz.org. Preliminary name searches and name reservations are no longer available from the Division of Corporations. You are responsible for any name infringement that may result from your name selection.

NOTE: This form for filing Articles of Organization is basic. Each limited liability company is a separate entity and as such has specific goals, needs, and requirements. Additionally, the tax consequences arising from the structure of a limited liability company can be significant. The Division of Corporations recommends that all documents be reviewed by your legal counsel. The Division is a filing agency and as such does not render any legal, accounting, or tax advice. The professional advice of your legal counsel to ascertain exact compliance with all statutory requirements is strongly recommended.

Pursuant to s. 608.407, Florida Statutes, the Articles of Organization must set forth the following:

ARTICLE I:
The name of the limited liability company, which **must** end with the words "Limited Liability Company," the abbreviation "L.L.C.," or the designation "LLC." (The word "limited" may be abbreviated as "Ltd." and the word "company" may be abbreviated as "Co.")

ARTICLE II:
The mailing address and the street address of the principal office of the limited liability company.

ARTICLE III:
The name and Florida street address of the limited liability company's registered agent. The registered agent must sign and state that he/she is familiar with and accepts the obligations of the position.

ARTICLE IV:
The name and address of each Manager or Managing member. Insert "MGR" for each Manager. Insert "MGRM" for each Managing Member. IMPORTANT: Most financial institutions require this information to be recorded with the Florida Department of State.

CR2E047 (09/10)

ARTICLE V:
If an effective date is listed, the date must be specific and cannot be more than five business days prior to or 90 days after the date of filing.

What is an effective date?
You may list an effective date if you would like the limited liability company's existence to become effective on a date other than the date it is filed by this office., The effective date can be up to 5 business days prior to the date of receipt or up to 90 days after the date of receipt.

The entity's first annual report form will be due January 1st of the calendar year following the year of formation. If a limited liability company is created late in the calendar year and it doesn't expect to commence business until on or after January 1st of the upcoming year, it should add an effective date of January 1 for the coming year.

If the effective date is in the next calendar year, it will delay the requirement to file an annual report until the following calendar year. Example: A limited liability company is formed December 1, 2007. if it added an effective date of January 1, 2008, the first annual report would not be due until January 1, 2009. If a 2008 effective was not listed, the first annual report would be due January 1, 2008.

Signature:
Articles of Organization must be executed by at least one member or authorized representative of a member, and the execution of the document constitutes an affirmation under the penalties of perjury that the facts stated therein are true.

FILING FEES:
$125.00   Filing Fee for Articles of Organization and Designation of Registered Agent
$ 30.00   Certified Copy (optional)
$ 5.00   Certificate of Status (optional)

A letter of acknowledgment will be issued free of charge upon registration. Please submit one check made payable to the Florida Department of State for the total amount of the filing fees and any optional certificate or copy.

A cover letter containing your name, address and daytime telephone number should be submitted along with the articles of organization and the check. The mailing address and courier address are:

Mailing Address	Street/Courier Address
Registration Section	Registration Section
Division of Corporations	Division of Corporations
P.O. Box 6327	Clifton Building
Tallahassee, FL 32314	2661 Executive Center Circle
(850)245-6051	Tallahassee, FL 32301
	(850)245-6051

Important Information About the Requirement to File an Annual Report
All Florida Limited Liability Companies must file an Annual Report yearly to maintain "active" status. The first report is due in the year <u>following</u> formation. The report must be filed electronically online between January 1st and May 1st. The fee for the annual report is $138.75. After May 1st a $400 late fee is added to the annual report filing fee. "Annual Report Reminder Notices" are sent to the e-mail address you provide us when you submit this document for filing. To file any time after January 1st, go to our website at www.sunbiz.org. There is no provision to waive the late fee. Be sure to file before May 1st.

Any further inquiries concerning this matter should be directed to the Registration Section by calling (850)245-6051.

COVER LETTER

TO: Registration Section
　　　Division of Corporations

SUBJECT: _____
　　　　　　　　　　　(Name of Limited Liability Company)

The enclosed Articles of Organization and fee(s) are submitted for filing.

Please return all correspondence concerning this matter to the following:

_____
(Name of Person)

_____
(Firm/Company)

_____
(Address)

_____
(City/State and Zip Code)

_____
E-mail address: (to be used for future annual report notification)

For further information concerning this matter, please call:

_____ at (_____)_____
　(Name of Person)　　　　(Area Code & Daytime Telephone Number)

Enclosed is a check for the following amount:

☐ $125.00 Filing Fee ☐ $130.00 Filing Fee & Certificate of Status ☐ $155.00 Filing Fee & Certified Copy (additional copy is enclosed) ☐ $160.00 Filing Fee, Certificate of Status & Certified Copy (additional copy is enclosed)

MAILING ADDRESS:
Registration Section
Division of Corporations
P.O. Box 6327
Tallahassee, FL 32314

STREET/COURIER ADDRESS:
Registration Section
Division of Corporations
Clifton Building
2661 Executive Center Circle
Tallahassee, FL 32301

ARTICLES OF ORGANIZATION FOR FLORIDA LIMITED LIABILITY COMPANY

ARTICLE I - Name:
The name of the Limited Liability Company is:

_____
(Must end with the words "Limited Liability Company," "L.L.C.," or "LLC.")

ARTICLE II - Address:
The mailing address and street address of the principal office of the Limited Liability Company is:

Principal Office Address: **Mailing Address:**

_____   _____

_____   _____

_____   _____

ARTICLE III - Registered Agent, Registered Office, & Registered Agent's Signature:
(The Limited Liability Company cannot serve as its own Registered Agent. You must designate an individual or another business entity with an active Florida registration.)

The name and the Florida street address of the registered agent are:

_____
Name

_____
Florida street address (P.O. Box **NOT** acceptable)

_____FL_____
City, State, and Zip

Having been named as registered agent and to accept service of process for the above stated limited liability company at the place designated in this certificate, I hereby accept the appointment as registered agent and agree to act in this capacity. I further agree to comply with the provisions of all statutes relating to the proper and complete performance of my duties, and I am familiar with and accept the obligations of my position as registered agent as provided for in Chapter 608, F.S..

_____
Registered Agent's Signature (REQUIRED)

(CONTINUED)
Page 1 of 2

ARTICLE IV- Manager(s) or Managing Member(s):
The name and address of each Manager or Managing Member is as follows:

Title:
"MGR" = Manager
"MGRM" = Managing Member

Name and Address:

_____   _____
                                   _____
                                   _____
_____   _____
                                   _____
                                   _____
_____   _____
                                   _____
                                   _____
_____   _____
                                   _____

(Use attachment if necessary)

ARTICLE V: Effective date, if other than the date of filing:_____.
(OPTIONAL)
(If an effective date is listed, the date must be specific and cannot be more than five business days prior to or 90 days after the date of filing.)

REQUIRED **SIGNATURE:**

_____
Signature of a member or sin authorized representative of a member.

(In accordance with section 608.408(3), Florida Statutes, the execution of this document constitutes an affirmation under the penalties of perjury that the facts stated herein are true. I am aware that any false information submitted in a document to the Department of State constitutes a third degree felony as provided for in s.817.155, F.S.)

_____
Typed or printed name of signee

Filing Fees:
$125.00 Filing Fee for Articles of Organization and Designation of Registered Agent
$ 30.00 Certified Copy (Optional)
$ 5.00 Certificate of Status (Optional)

FLORIDA DEPARTMENT OF STATE
DIVISION OF CORPORATIONS

INSTRUCTIONS FOR A PROFIT CORPORATION

The following are instructions, a cover letter and sample articles of incorporation pursuant to Chapter 607 and 621 Florida Statutes (F.S.).

NOTE: THIS IS A BASIC FORM MEETING MINIMAL REQUIREMENTS FOR FILING ARTICLES OF INCORPORATION.

The Division of Corporations strongly recommends that corporate documents be reviewed by your legal counsel. The Division is a filing agency and as such does not render any legal, accounting, or tax advice.

This office does not provide you with corporate seals, minute books, or stock certificates. It is the responsibility of the corporation to secure these items once the corporation has been filed with this office.

Questions concerning S Corporations should be directed to the Internal Revenue Service by telephoning 1-800-829-1040. This is an IRS designation, which is not determined by this office.

A preliminary search for name availability can be made on the Internet through the Division's records at www.sunbiz.org. Preliminary name searches and name reservations are no longer available from the Division of Corporations. You are responsible for any name infringement that may result from your corporate name selection.

Pursuant to Chapter 607 or 621 F.S., the articles of incorporation **must** set forth the following:

Article I: The name of the corporation **must** include a corporate suffix such as Corporation, Corp., Incorporated, Inc., Company, or Co.

A Professional Association **must** contain the word "chartered" or "professional association" or "P.A.".

Article II: The principal place of business and mailing address of the corporation. The principal address must be a **street** address. The mailing address, if different, can be a P.O. Box address.

Article III: **Specific Purpose for a "Professional Corporation"**

Article IV: The number of shares of stock that this corporation is authorized to have **must** be stated.

CR2E010 (11/09)"

Article V: The names, address and titles of the Directors/Officers **(optional).** The names of officers/directors may be required to apply for a license, open a bank account, etc.

Article VI: The name and **Florida Street address** (P.O. Box **NOT** acceptable) of the initial Registered Agent. The Registered Agent **must** sign in the space provided and type or print his/her name accepting the designation as registered agent.

Article VII: The name and address of the Incorporator, The Incorporator must sign in the space provided and type or print his/her name below signature.

An Effective Date: Add a separate **article if applicable or necessary:** An effective date may be added to the Articles of Incorporation, otherwise the date of receipt will be the file date. (An effective date can not be more than five (5) business days prior to the date of receipt or ninety (90) days after the date of filing). **If a corporation is filed anytime prior to December 31st, an annual report will be due on January 1st.**

***

The fee for filing a profit corporation is:

Filing Fee	$35.00
Designation of Registered Agent	$35.00
Certified Copy (optional)	$ 8.75 (plus $1 per page for each page over 8, not to exceed a maximum of $52.50).
Certificate of Status (optional)	$ 8.75

Make checks payable to: Florida Department of State

<u>**Mailing Address:**</u>
Department of State
Division of Corporations
P.O. Box 6327
Tallahassee, FL 32314
(850) 245-6052

<u>**Street Address:**</u>
Department of State
Division of Corporations
Clifton Building
2661 Executive Center Circle
Tallahassee, FL 32301
(850) 245-6052

COVER LETTER

Department of State
New Filing Section
Division of Corporations
P. O. Box 6327
Tallahassee, FL 32314

SUBJECT: _____
(PROPOSED CORPORATE NAME – <u>MUST INCLUDE SUFFIX</u>)

Enclosed are an original and one (1) copy of the articles of incorporation and a check for:

☐ $70.00 Filing Fee

☐ $78.75 Filing Fee & Certificate of Status

☐ $78.75 Filing Fee & Certified Copy

☐ $87.50 Filing Fee, Certified Copy & Certificate of Status

ADDITIONAL COPY REQUIRED

_____
Name (Printed or typed)

_____
(Address)

_____
City, State and Zip

_____
Daytime Telephone number

_____
E-mail address: (to be used for future annual report notification)

NOTE: Please provide the original and one copy of the articles.

CORPORATIONS

ARTICLES OF INCORPORATION
In compliance with Chapter 607 and/or Chapter 621, F.S. (Profit)

ARTICLE I   NAME
The name of the corporation shall be:

ARTICLE II   PRINCIPAL OFFICE
The principal street address and mailing address, if different is:

ARTICLE III   PURPOSE
The purpose for which the corporation is organized is:

ARTICLE IV   SHARES
The number of shares of stock is:

ARTICLE V   INITIAL OFFICERS AND/OR DIRECTORS
List name(s), address(es) and specific title(s):

ARTICLE VI   REGISTERED AGENT
The name and Florida street address (P.O. Box **NOT** acceptable) of the registered agent is:

ARTICLE VII   INCORPORATOR
The name and address of the Incorporator is:

****

Having been named as registered agent to accept service of process for the above stated corporation at the place designated in this certificate, I am familiar with and accept the appointment as registered agent and agree to act in this capacity

_____   _____
Signature/Registered Agent   Date

_____   _____
Signature/Registered Agent   Date

CORPORATE BANK RESOLUTION

PURSUANT TO THE BYLAWS OF _(corporation)_, A _(State of Inc.)_ **CORPORATION**, which has Resoluted that the Undersigned be Authorized and Directed to open a Corporate Checkings and Savings Account in its Registered Name, and any other accounts as is needed by the Corporation; and be Granted the power to deposit and withdraw all funds, drafts, checks, notes, etc. of the corporation.

(Corp. Name) was Incorporated with The Department of State, Division of Corporation, Leon County, Tallahassee, Florida on the _____ day of _____ 201_____.

A Certified Copy of its Articles of Incorporation and Certificate of Status is submitted herewith; along with the Corporation's EIN Number.

RESOLVED, that _(Name & Title of Officer)_ be Authorized, Directed and Granted sole Power to execute all documents, instruments, Resolutions and or any other Documents associated and or necessary with the operations of said Corporate Account; and to be Granted Authority to Direct other Officials access to said account as necessary.

FURTHER RESOLVED, that the signing of this RESOLUTION by _(Name & Title of Officer)_ shall constitute Full Ratification thereof.

RATIFIED THIS _____ DAY OF _____ 201 _____.

(Name & Title of Corporation Officer)

CORP.   SEAL

AFTER INCORPORATION

After Incorporating either your LLC or corporations I suggest the following steps:

1. Contact the IRS after receiving your "Certificate of Status" from your Secretary of State, and request a form 'SS-4.' The form is free and immediately after filling it out, you will be issued a EIN number specifically for your corporation. This will be your corporation's tax i.d. number.

The IRS's website is www.irs.gov;

2. Stop soonafter to the nearest Office Depot and purchase a "Corporate Kit." This consists of your corporate minutes, Resolutions, corporate seal, bylaws, and stock certificate. These documents are needed for your annually held shareholders meeting, which is due to your Secretary of State's office before the end of your calendar-decided year;

3. Within your 'corporate kit,' spell out your duties and the duties of any employees should you decide to hire any. Spell out any and all resolutions that the company shall be bounded by; including how it is to operate, who shall call meetings, how are conflicts decided, who shall be responsible for writing checks and banking affairs, etc.

4. Issue yourself 75,000 shares of the C corporation or 75% of the LLC, for your sweat equity and contributions to the LLC that consists of Copyrights, domain names, ideas, drafts, designs, sketches, plans, trademarks, etc.

Value those shaves at 0.001 cent and document the transfer within your Resolutions and corporate minute book. Be sure to place a copy of the stock certificate within the "Schedules."

5. Draft a "corporate Bank Resolution" after you determine who will be responsible for dealing with the corporation's banking affairs (remember, you can appoint yourself), then authorize the opening of a checkings and savings account.

Use the checkings account **solely** as the corporation's main operating account, for any pass through monies (this means when you're receiving profits, paying bills, overhead and other expenses.

Use the savings account for profits and savings.
Be sure to document these Resolutions within your corporate minute book as well, including a copy of the original document;

6. Find a bookstore and purchase a book on the field subject of "how to run your own corporation";

7. Obtain the necessary business license from your county's tax collectors office or your local state courthouse;

8. After completing your corporate kit and rapping up your initial shareholder's meeting, mail the original minutes to The Secretary of State. Tour next annual meeting won't be held until the following year on or before the same date.

Said hearing will consist of documenting everything that transpired regarding the corporation in the previous year;

9. **Keep every** receipt and deduct **every** expense you can tie to the corporation;

10. And conduct every single business in the corporation's name, even if its a birthday party.

DON'T FORGET, that while you're preparing your annual minutes, that you have to sell the corporation its copyrights, trademarks, domain name(s), sketches, designs, ideas, and any other intellectual and tangible property in your possession that may be useful to the corporation.

In exchange, the corporation is pledging to issues you 75,000 shares of the C corporation, and or 75% of the LLC, in addition to a one million dollar Promissory Note, payable on first demand.

It is of most **Paramount importance** that you document this as well in your corporate minute book prior to mailing off to your Secretary of State. **You must** draft a contract transferring the property from your personal capacity, to that of the corporation. And be sure to stamp all documents and titles in the corporation's stamp and seal, showing its ownership.

On the next page is a SS-4 form (Application for EIN number).

Form SS-4
(Rev. January 2010)

Department of the Treasury
Internal Revenue Service

Application for Employer Identification Number

(For use by employers, corporations, partnerships, trusts, estates, churches, government agencies, Indian tribal entities, certain individuals, and others.)

▶ See separate instructions for each line.   ▶ Keep a copy for your records.

OMB No. 1545-0003

EIN

Type or print clearly.

1 Legal name of entity (or individual) for whom the EIN is being requested

2 Trade name of business (if different from name on line 1)

3 Executor, administrator, trustee, "care of" name

4a Mailing address (room, apt., suite no. and street, or P.O. box)

5a Street address (if different) (Do not enter a P.O. box.)

4b City, state, and ZIP code (if foreign, see instructions)

5b City, state, and ZIP code (if foreign, see instructions)

6 County and state where principal business is located

7a Name of responsible party

7b SSN, (TIN, or EIN

8a Is this application for a limited liability company (LLC) (or a foreign equivalent)? . . . . ☐ Yes ☐ No

8b If 8a is "Yes," enter the number of LLC members . . . . . . ▶

8c If 8a is "Yes," was the LLC organized in the United States? . . . . ☐ Yes ☐ No

9a Type of entity (check only one box). Caution. If 8a is "Yes," see the instructions for the correct box to check.
☐ Sole proprietor (SSN) _____
☐ Partnership
☐ Corporation (enter form number to be filed) ▶ _____
☐ Personal service corporation
☐ Church or church-controlled organization
☐ Other nonprofit organization (specify) ▶ _____
☐ Other (specify) ▶

☐ Estate (SSN of decedent) _____
☐ Plan administrator (TIN) _____
☐ Trust (TIN of grantor) _____
☐ National Guard   ☐ State/local government
☐ Farmers' cooperative ☐ Federal government/military
☐ REMIC   ☐ Indian tribal governments/enterprises
Group Exemption Number (GEN) if any ▶

9b If a corporation, name the state or foreign country (if applicable) where incorporated

State	Foreign country

10 **Reason for applying** (check only one box)
☐ Started new business (specify type) ▶ _____
☐ Hired employees (Check the box and see line 13.)
☐ Compliance with IRS withholding regulations
☐ Other (specify) ▶

☐ Banking purpose (specify purpose) ▶ _____
☐ Changed type of organization (specify new type) ▶ _____
☐ Purchased going business
☐ Created a trust (specify type) ▶ _____
☐ Created a pension plan (specify type) ▶ _____

11 Date business started or acquired (month, day, year). See instructions.

12 Closing month of accounting year

13 Highest number of employees expected in the next 12 months (enter -0- if none). If no employees expected, skip line 14.

Agricultural	Household	Other

14 If you expect your employment tax liability to be $1,000 or less in a full calendar year **and** want to file Form 944 annually instead of Forms 941 quarterly, check here. (Your employment tax liability generally will be $1,000 or less if you expect to pay $4,000 or less in total wages.) If you do not check this box, you must file Form 941 for every quarter.

15 First date wages or annuities were paid (month, day, year). **Note.** If applicant is a withholding agent, enter date income will first be paid to nonresident alien (month, day, year)...▶

16 Check one box that best describes the principal activity of your business. ☐ Health care & social assistance ☐ Wholesale-agent/broker
☐ Construction   ☐ Rental & leasing ☐ Transportation & warehousing   ☐ Accommodation & food service ☐ Wholesale-other ☐ Retail
☐ Real estate   ☐ Manufacturing   ☐ Finance & insurance   ☐ Other (specify)

17 Indicate principal line of merchandise sold, specific construction work done, products produced, or services provided.

18 Has the applicant entity shown on line 1 ever applied for and received an EIN? ☐ Yes ☐ No
If "Yes," write previous EIN here ▶

Third Party Designee	Complete this section **only** if you want to authorize the named individual to receive the entity's EIN and answer questions about the completion of this form.	
	Designee's name	Designee's telephone number (include area code) ( )
	Address and ZIP code	Designee's fax number (include area code) ( )

Under penalties of perjury, I declare that I have examined this application, and to the best of my knowledge and belief, it is true, correct, and complete.

Name and title (type or print clearly) ▶

Designee's telephone number (include area code)
( )

Signature ▶   Date ▶

Designee's fax number (include area code)
( )

For Privacy Act and Paperwork Reduction Act Notice, see separate instructions.   Cat. No. 16055N   Form **SS-4** (Rev. 1-2010)

FICTITIOUS NAMES

Another thing to add underneath your thinking cap is how to familiarize yourself with and use fictitious names, which is another term for 'doing business as' (dba).

The need for a fictitious name is when a company is incorporated, but may want to additionally conduct business in other branches or areas consistent with the 'purpose' definitions set out in Article III of the Incorporation application.

For Example: say you incorporate 'Entertainment, Express, Inc.' and your purpose of incorporating is in all fields of non sensored adult entertainment. Your primary business consists of booking: shows, acts, entertainers, artists, and models.

But now you want to open a studio. So what you would do is register what is known as a fictitious name for the studio to do business in, like 'Studio Hits.' When approved, the company is now doing business in a fictitious name because its parent company is 'Entertainment Express, Inc.'

Now notice, that 'Studio Hit Factory' did not have to go back through the incorporating process. All it had to do was register as a fictitious name with its Secretary Department of State. The protection lasts for five years and costs $80.00 for the Certificate of Status and the Certified Copy.

You can file a fictitious name for all business that you list as your purpose to conduct business in. If it has a different purpose than what you initially listed in the Articles of Incorporation, then you have to re-incorporate.

HOW TO FILE A FICITIOUS NAME

1. See if the domain name is available. Pretty much if the domain name is available then so is the name you want to use;

2. Pay for a newspaper publication in the biggest newspaper that primarily circulates in your city. Pay for it to run at least one day;

3. Make a copy of the receipts and attach them with the registration application that I have supplied hereafter, along with a U.S. Postal money order for the amount of $80.00

4. When the Certificate of Status and Certified copy is mailed back to you, then take both of them down to your state county courthouse and file them with the clerk's office, to be viewed as public information.

Instructions for Completing Application for Registration of Fictitious Name

Section 1: **Line 1**: Enter the name as you wish it to be registered. A fictitious name may <u>not</u> contain the words "Corporation" or "Incorporated," or the abbreviations "Corp." or "Inc.," unless the person or business for which the name is registered is incorporated or has obtained a certificate of authority to transact business in this state pursuant to chapter 607 or chapter 617 Florida Statutes. Corporations are not required to file under their exact corporate name.

Line 2: Enter the mailing address of the business. This address does not have to be the principal place of business and can be directed to anyone's attention. DO NOT USE AN ADDRESS THAT IS NOT YET OCCUPIED. ALL FUTURE MAILINGS AND ANY CERTIFICATION REQUESTED ON THIS REGISTRATION FORM WILL BE SENT TO THE ADDRESS IN SECTION 1. An address may be changed at any future date with no charge by simply writing the Division.

Line 3: Enter the name of the county in Florida where the principal place of business of the fictitious name is located. If there is more than one county, list all applicable counties or state "multiple".

Line 4: Enter the Federal Employer Identification (FEI) number if known or if applicable. Please do not enter your social security number.

Section 2: **Part A:** Complete if the owner(s) of the fictitious name are individuals. The individual's name and address must be provided.

Part B: Complete if the owner(s) are not individuals. Examples are a corporation, limited partnership, joint venture, general partnership, trusts, fictitious name, etc. Provide the name of the owner, their address, their document number as registered with the Division of Corporations, and the Federal Employer Identification (FEI) number. An FEI number must be provided or the appropriate box must be checked.

Owners listed in Part B must be registered with the Division of Corporations or provide documentation as to why they are not required to register. Examples would be Federally Chartered Corporations, or Legislatively created entities.

Additional owners may be listed on an attached page as long as all of the information requested in Part A or Part B is provided.

Section 3: Only one signature is required. It is preferred that a daytime phone number be provided in order to contact the applicant if there are any questions about the application.

Section 4: **TO CANCEL A REGISTRATION ON FILE:** Provide fictitious name, date filed, and registration number of the fictitious name to be cancelled.

TO CHANGE OWNERSHIP OF A REGISTRATION: Complete section 4 to cancel the original registration. Complete sections 1 through 3 to re-register the fictitious name listing the new owner(s). An owner's signature is required in both sections 3 and 4.

TO CHANGE THE NAME OF A REGISTRATION: Complete section 4 to cancel the original registration. Complete sections 1 through 3 to re-register the new fictitious name. An owner's signature is required in both sections 3 and 4.

An acknowledgement letter will be mailed when the fictitious name registration has been filed. The acknowledgement letter and any certification requested will be mailed to the address provided in Section 1. For **Cancellations Only:** please provide a mailing address on an attachment, if the address on our records is no longer valid. To request a certificate of status and/or certified copy, please check the appropriate box(es) and include the additional fee(s) ($10 for a certificate of status, $30 for a certified copy).

The registration and reregistration will be in effect until December 31 of the fifth year.

Send completed application with appropriate fees to:
Fictitious Name Registration
PO Box 1300
Tallahassee, FL 32302-1300

Internet Address:
http://www.sunbiz.org

Courier Address,
Division of Corporations
Clifton Building
2661 Executive Center Circle
Tallahassee, FL 32301

The fee for registering a fictitious name is $50. Please make a separate check for each filing payable to the Department of State. Application must be typed or printed in ink and legible.

Single CR4E001 (11/09)

APPLICATION FOR REGISTRATION OF FICTITIOUS NAME

Note: Acknowledgements/certificates will be sent to the address in Section 1 only.

Section 1

1. _____
   Fictitious Name to be Registered (see instructions if name includes "Corp" or "Inc")

   _____
   Mailing Address of Business

   _____
   City   State   Zip Code

3. Florida County of principal place of business: _____
   _____
   (see instructions if more than one county)

   FEI Number: _____

   This space for office use only

Section 2

A. Owner(s) of Fictitious Name If Individual(s): (Use an attachment if necessary):

1. _____   2. _____
   Last   First   M.I   Last   First   M.I

   _____   _____
   Address   Address

   _____   _____
   City   State   Zip Code   City   State   Zip Code

B. Owner(s) of Fictitious Name If other than an individual: (Use attachment if necessary):

1. _____   2. _____
   Last   First   M.I   Last   First   M.I

   _____   _____
   Address   Address

   _____   _____
   City   State   Zip Code   City   State   Zip Code

   Florida Document Number _____   Florida Document Number _____
   FEI Number: _____   FEI Number: _____
   ☐ Applied for   ☐ Not Applicable   ☐ Applied for   ☐ Not Applicable

Section 3

I the undersigned, being an owner in the above fictitious name, certify that the information indicated on this form is true and accurate. In accordance with Section 865.09, F.S., I further certify that the fictitious name to be registered has been advertised at least once in a newspaper as defined in chapter 50, Florida Statutes, in the county where the principal place of business is located. I understand that the signature below shall have the same legal effect as if made under oath.

_____   _____
Signature of Owner   Date   E-mail address: (to be used for future renewal notification)

Phone Number: _____

Section 4

FOR CANCELLATION COMPLETE SECTION 4 ONLY:
FOR FICTITIOUS NAME OR OWNERSHIP CHANGE COMPLETE SECTIONS 1 THROUGH 4:

I (we) the undersigned, hereby cancel the fictitious name _____ which was registered on _____ and was assigned registration number _____

_____   _____
Signature of Owner   Date   Signature of Owner   Date

Mark the applicable boxes   ☐ Certificate of Status — $10   ☐ Certified Copy — $30

NON-REFUNDABLE PROCESSING FEE: $50   Single   CR4E001 (11/09)

BE YOUR OWN CEO OR GENERAL MANAGER AND RUN YOUR OWN COMPANY OR CORPORATION

RUN YOUR OWN COMPANY OR CORPORATION

If you had been paying attention to anything I've been telling you then you're already the Chairman of your corporation. This means that you are the majority shareholder and shot caller of the business. This was the plan that you designed wasn't it? And there is no greater feeling in America than owning a corporation, its part of the American Dream.

But what good is it if you can't make it pay you, or benefit from it? The greatest feeling is owning the corporation. The greatness of the feeling is for it to be profitable. Think about the ones that are, and when you do you think of the Goliath companies. And even when they first incorporated, they visioned being where they are today. You can be your own CEO and Managing Member, and at the same time, run your own corporation. You can control the destiny of the company first hand. All that is required is that you be hands on regarding the company's day to day activities **(remember what I said earlier though, depending on the business, if you're a convicted felon then this isn't wise. However, it isn't non advisable).**

One of the best and truest quotes still remain: "If you want something done right, sometimes its worth doing it yourself." If investing blood, sweat, years and tears in your corporation Grants you an excited adrenaline worth feigning, then go for it! You'll learn alot, mature in the process and be privy to an experience you'll never forget.

HOWEVER, there's Rules that Govern your way into becoming successful in your mission. I like to call them "The 10 Keys to Success." Follow me as I walk you through them:

1. VISION

Its hard to overcome business challenges with an employee mentality. Every CEO must have a clear vision for his company; and it must be effectively and consistently communicated to each employee. You have to envision where the company is going and in which direction it is headed.

2. RECRUIT SMARTER PEOPLE THAN YOURSELF

To propel your company to a farfetched level, you have to identify the right co-pilots. It takes more than evaluating resumes and calling references. It takes reaching outside of your comfort zone, hiding your ego and selecting those that you would normally feel intimidated of. You have alot to learn from them; and alot to teach them as well.

3. A POWERHOUSE MANAGEMENT TEAM

Identifying and selecting more knowledgeable, smarter and skilled talent is only part of the equation. Unifying them as a cohesive team within your company is another. It takes more than the intelligence of a single individual to sometimes make it to another level. Powerhouse Management teams represents one of the most essential factors in a company's success.

4. LIMITATIONS

Sometimes, a company's success is also determined by its limitations. A CEO can sometimes reach a point to where his decisions may sometimes impair the business. Take a long look in the mirror. Allow your powerhouse team to pull certain triggers, in the name of risk. In the end, the company will be known for such bold moves.

5. NETWORK

CEOs must build a solid network. The developement of a powerful network is needed to expand. Therefore, networking should be maximumized to its fullest extent, even if you're not networking in the field of your company.

6. GLOBALIZE

CEOs should step out of their box and reach across international borders. Global business is a huge market for companies that havn't tapped into them. Learn import/export and network globally and you'll find that international markets are just as anxious to network and do business with you, as you are them.

7. CHECKINGS AND SAVINGS ACCOUNT

When establishing your bank accounts, you should always have one as a checkings and one as a savings. Use the checkings account as your main operating account. This account is used for everything under the sun that regards the corporation. When everything is paid from this account, transfer all profits to the savings account. Banks or other creditors won't be able to tap into this account for any funds, reimbursements, etc. if the savings account is accurately Governed.

8. PAY FOR NOTHING IN CASH

Whatever you do, PAY FOR NOTHING IN CASH!
Everything should be paid **(EVERYTHING)** by the corporation credit card. Cash should only be paid to the credit card companies if you're not transfering the funds from your checkings account.
Carrying out this method boosts the company's credit report and credit score, when applying for future loans.

9. MENTOR TO THE NEXT GENERATION OF YOUR SEEDS

Your younger Generational seeds should be mentored as you lead the company on to its road of up and coming success. If groomed properly, they'll take over as family leaders who'll be in better positions to lead the company with fresh perspectives, technological innovation and entree to new markets.

10. DEVELOPE AN EXIT STRATEGY

Always start with the end in mind, even if the end consists of passing the company down to the next in line. It coincides with the most important and introspective question that exist: What was I aiming for when creating the company? The truest thing ever spoke was: "meet your goals, meet other goals, then live your dreams."

With these ten points in mind, there's no reason why your company shouldn't prosper in whatever field you set out to operate in. Use these same key points in mind while operating your company and watch it provide for you and your families to come.

REGISTERING WITH DUN & BRADSTREET

DUN & BRADSTREET

Registering your company is just one stage closer to professionalism. The next is to get it registered with a accredited credit bureau. This is where Dun & Bradstreet come into perspective.

Bun & Bradstreet is the King Kong for credit reporting on companies and corporations. They store data on millions of businesses. A few of their services are:

a. Charging vendors to pull credit reports;
b. Charging you to build a credit report on your business;
c. Charging businesses to pull credit on other businesses;
d. And charging creditors to pull credit reports on seemingly irresponsible businesses.

They also have a multitude of other services like credit monitoring; credit investigations; and data base retrieval, wherein they search existing businesses credit reports to find suitable new clients and etc.

Some companies pull reports on businesses before purchasing them or investing in them. This makes Dun & Bradstreet not only an outstanding credit Bureau, but a valuable resource which is a necessity in its own right. And because of such, Banks approve major loans on their reports alone.

So read carefully as I guide you through the registering process of securing your Dun & Bradstreet number.

The first thing you need to do to register, is go online to: http://www.dnb.com/eupdate and apply for a Dun & Bradstreet "credit Builder's service."

The service runs for approximately $500 – $600 dollars, and the entire questionnaire is done online.

The questionnaire is easy and strait forward to use. It'll ask you when and what city and state the business was formed in; how many employees, if you have any; what type of services you provide; the name, titles and number of employees the company have; the key officers educational background and job experiences; key employees job descriptions; the company's name, business and email address; the company's legal structure and whether its publicly traded or not; whether the company is owned by another company or corporation; and the company's means of operations. Sometimes, it even requests the number of customers the company has, how payment is accepted from them, and the service area that the company covers.

When filing out the questionnaire, you may choose to ignore any shareholder information and 'year current owners' questions, as well as who your customers are.

Dun & Bradstreet will sometimes request that you fax or email them a copy of your company's financials; and sometimes, to provide them with at least 5 references. But don't trip if you don't have any references at this time, once you have paid for the 'credit builder' service, you have 6 months to obtain at least 5 references to your company's credit report. They'll assist you in utilizing those references you choose to do business with.

After everything is completed regarding the questionnaire, Dun & Bradstreet will generate a 'D-U-N-S' number for your corporation within 24 hours (excluding holidays and weekends). They will also send you an automatic email confirmation with a user name and password so you can log on to 'eupdate' and review your reports yourself. Just do not log on more than once a month, or your business will be placed in a high-risk category.

However, once you're registered with Dun & Bradstreet, keep good standing regarding your credit with the various companies you deal with. You'll find that the better your credit remains, with the simpliest orders, the greater your chances are for your company to be provided unsecured loans and or unsecured credit lines.

This proves very useful when you attain the mindset of using others money to make money, without risking your own. There's a great deal of companies that scan Dun & Bradstreet's database searching for companies with good credit histories. Such companies that are discovered, enjoy the privilege to call up a variety of companies and place an order on deferred payment plans. And when said agreements are abided by, then the limits keeps growing.

I have supplied, as close as I possibly could, an online registry questionnaire of essential things asked of you by Dun and Bradstreet, when securing a Duns number.

http://eupdate.dnb.com/eupdate.asp

Dun & Bradstreet Credit Builder®

Begin Creating a D&B Number/Report

Your First Name:

Your Last Name:

Your Title:

Your Email Address:

Company Telephone:

Submit

http://eupdate.dnb.com/eupdate.asp

Dun & Bradstreet Credit Builder®

Company Information

Name of Business:	This is the full legal name of your corporation.
Other Names:	Any other names your corporation is known by.
Business Address:	This must be a commercial or retail address. Avoid using a residential address! Use your virtual office address if you have one.
City:	
State:	
Zip Code:	
Local Phone No.:	
Toll Free Phone No.:	
Company Fax No.:	
Mailing Address:	Use this only if you have a separate billing address, such as a P.O. Box.
Number:	
City:	
State:	
Zip Code:	

Next

Another Company Owns More than 50% of this Business:

Prnt. Company Name: [   ]

Prnt. Company City: [   ]

Prnt. Company State: [   ]

Prnt. Company Cntry: [   ]

> Use this section only if your company is owned by another company, most small business owners may skip this section.

Next

---

http://eupdate.dnb.com/eupdate.asp

Dun & Bradstreet Credit Builder®

Management

Name Offcr./Ownr.: [   ]

Title: [   ]

Other: [   ]

Areas of Resp.: [   ]

Started With Co.: [   ]

> This is a drop down list. Choose the appropriate areas. Hold down the CNTRL key on your keyboard to select more than one (one).

Add Principal

> Click here to add more principal employees.

Next

REGISTERING WITH DUN & BRADSTREET

http://eupdate.dnb.com/eupdate.asp

Dun & Bradstreet Credit Builder®

Work Experience

Name of Business:

Year of Birth:

From:

To:

Company Name:

City:

State:

Foreign Country:

Not Active in Daily:

Education

Year Graduated:

Degree:

Graduated From:

College Attended:

> This will be repeated for each officer, owner, or director listed previously.

Save

http://eupdate.dnb.com/eupdate.asp

Dun & Bradstreet Credit Builder®

Operations

Primary Line of Bus.: [ ]

Total No. of Empl.: [ ] — This is the total number of employees in all locations.

Additional Co. Loc.: [ ]

No. Employ. At HQ: [ ]

How do you bill your customers: (Check all that apply.)

Cash, Check, & Credit Card:
Net 7 Days:
Net 10 Days:
Net 15 Days:
Net 30 Days:
one% Net 30 Days:
2% Net 30 Days:
Retainer, Plus:
Contractual:
Fee:
Require Deposit, Billed:
Commission:
Seasonal:

— Check all the ways that your customers pay you.

Number of Active Credit Accounts: [ ] — The number of customers you invoice every month.
Check here if you sell on the Internet: [ ]

% of Sales from the Internet: [ ]

Selling or Service Area:
Check here if you export:

(Continued Next Page)

http://eupdate.dnb.com/eupdate.asp

Dun & Bradstreet Credit Builder®

Ownership

Name of

Title: — *This is a drop down list; select the title that best describes the position of the CEO.*

If Other Enter Here:

Email Address:

Legal Structure:

List Shareholders: — *Ignore this question.*

Publicly Traded: — *Just answer yes or no. Most small businesses are not publicly traded.*

Year Business Started:

Year Current Owner: — *Ignore this question.*

Check all that apply:
More than 50% Woman Owned: ☐

More than 50% Minority Owned: ☐

Specify Minority:

Vietnam Veteran: ☐

Disabled Veteran: ☐

(Continued Next Page)

Your Customers
Describe who you sell to (Check all that apply.)

Manufacturers:
Wholesalers:
Retailers:
Government:
General Public:
Non-Profit Organizations:
Commercial Concerns:

> Select all the types of clients you sell to.

Primary Place of Business

Residence:
Commercial:

> Use the details from your virtual office, commercial, or retail space. Do not use residence details.

If residence, select from whose residence:

Square Footage:

Floor Number:

Number of Stories:

Type of Building:

Next

---

http://eupdate.dnb.com/eupdate.asp

Dun & Bradstreet Credit Builder®

Ownership

Expedited D-U-N-S™ Number $49.00

Purchase D&B Credit Builder™ $499.00

> Choose D&B's Expedited D-U-N-S Number service and you will be offered the Credit Builder Service on the next page. Then you will have the opportunity to add references to your file.

REGISTERING WITH DUN & BRADSTREET

Now here's some powerful info on the hush-hush so make certain you keep this on the low low. Dun & Bradstreet are not that all made out to be when it comes to thorough searches and investigations. They ultimately investigate whether or not the company is legit. So if your company is incorporated and has its EIN number, then pretty much everything else you submit to them when registering your company, is indisputable. What they do in turn, is sell that information to other companies who may inquire about your business, or whom may be interested in providing you a loan. Everything which is reported from the point of your business registration with them, is all that Dun & Bradstreet can verify. So setting up the best profile is key. Everything you enlist in the beginning is taken for credible value when you set up your profile, so keep your credibility in perfect standing once you secure investors and creditors looking to do business with you.

Below, I have provided the best scenario as possible to guide you in setting up one of the most attractive profiles ever:

1. When initially registering, NEVER provide any financial information, skip this area of registering;
2. Use strategic goals for the upcoming year of the money that your company could possibly generate;
3. List your debt as 0;
4. Do Not make your accounts payable person the same person as any other employee;
5. Other than yourself, use clean backgrounded people whom have been to college as other employees in different positions;
6. Be sure that no employee that you list, has a bankruptcy on their record;
7. List the company as having other branches in other cities. Name the cities;
8. List at least a number of 12 employees for every branch, totaled with the number of employees that you have listed in your local area;
9. State that the business has been operating at least 4 years prior to its incorporation. You will do this by listing that the business was operat-

ing prior as an "Unincorporated Business Organisation" pursuant to §619.9338 of the IRS Code.

Now, regardless of them trying to convince you otherwise, DO NOT purchase nor pay for their credit builder service. You'll get your Duns Number in 30 days regardless. They'll have employees calling and nagging you to purchase all sorts of programs to speed the process, but its all unnecessary.

CHAPTER 8
SECURING BUSINESS CREDIT

BUSINESS CREDIT

If you ever fully understood the importance of having good business credit then you'd come to terms that having it is more important than having personal credit.

We know that it doesn't take much to destroy your personal credit, but if you keep it in good standing, then there will be an unaccountable amounts of credit card agencies preapproving you credit limits, in hopes that you will pay them.

I don't know if anyone ever fully explained to you how credit work but the first and most important thing to know about it is that you're not getting anything for free. So when you think that a preaaproved credit card is free money, or a preapproved loan is free money then think again. Here's what just happened:

Say for instance that you're overloaded on stock and you need to find a buyer to get rid of it. This stock may be out of date, or out of trend. Now what happens is, I gotta get rid of this stock, but I can't afford to lose the money that I've purchased this stock with. So what I do is find customers whom believe that they could get rid of the stock, without paying their money for it. So I preapprove a line of credit for them and ship them the stock on face value. Now at this point, it really doesn't matter to me whether they sale the stock or not. Its there's and I want my money as soon as they get it. Even if it has to come from other inventory of theirs, that's not my problem.

You get the picture now? No one is doing you a favor by preapproving anything, unless your current position yells for it. With credit cards and credit lines, the game is a little difference. They're in the business of making money off of their money. So if they target someone whom is likely to pay them back, then they preapprove a credit limit for them and instantly they make a nice return off the interest. But how do they know? Lets look at how they arrive at their determinations:

PAYDEX SCORE

A "Paydex Score" and "Rating" of a business is generated by credit Bureaus to determine a business credit score. Usually, but not always, credit Bureaus requires references that are listed in their databases in order to initiate the process of your company's credit report. Those references are usually a bare minimum of 5 companies that you normally conduct business with. Here's the game on how it works:

A Paydex score is a specifically designed scoring system used by Dun & Bradstreet to evaluate how your company pays its bills. Its determined on the average of all of the company's financial responsibilities based on its dollar amounts.

To reflect a good score the company must usually pay its bigger bills on time and its smaller bills late. This is if the company manages to default on any of its bills in a timely manner. However, the company must at least try and timely pay all of the premiums set by the agencys.

Peep Game: The largest the monthly bills paid on time will guarantee the business a high credit score. The better the credit score, the more credit offered from a variety of other places.

In other words, make sure your largest monthly bills are paid at least 10 days ahead of time.

Now lets move on to "Rating."

RATING

The 'Rating' information is a specifically designed rating system that evaluate how financially stable a company is. It consists of the company's

"PADEX SCORE" and financial history, as evidenced by the company's financial report. This is evaluated by Banks and other lending companies. Essentially, the banks are really gawkers. They eye your company's daily account balance and match it with your 'paydex score.'

NSF Means 'Non Sufficient Funds' or a bad or bounced check.

There's really no need to work yourself up about this. This is just how banks rate you. If ever you wanted your company on a first name lending basis with banks from all over, then generate enough money with your company and keep at least 4 million dollars in the bank for your average balance. This will be extremely beautiful if your company's credit is outstanding.

However, in any event, keep your bills paid early or on time. This should be simple. Now lets move on to references:

REFERENCES

Be extremely careful when choosing references; and use only references that will boost your credit rating.

To obtain references, search Dun & Bradstreet database to determine the references that Dun & Bradstreet have listed. If you have no luck dealing with the references that Dun & Bradstreet provide then deal with highly accredited companies that otherwise: 1) offer commercial accounts; 2) offer net-30 terms (which allows you pay on its products within 30 days. In other words, 30 days credit lines); and report to Dun & Bradstreet directly.

Followed is a few vendors that may offer commercial accounts, 30-day net terms, and report directly to Dun & Bradstreet. Start with relative small orders; purchase from them a few times, approximately 5 months, then use them as a reference when completing your credit builder service.

Best But (www.bestbuy.com)
Kinkos (www.fedexkinkos.com)
Office Max (www.officemax.com)
Apple (www.apple.com)

Dell (www.dell.com)
Home Depot (www.homedepot.com)
Amazon (www.amazon.com)
Macys (www.macys.com)
Office Depot (www.officedepot.com)
Saks 5th Ave. (www.saks.com)
Target (www.target.com)
UPS (www.ups.com)
Verizon (www.verizon.com)
Walmart (www.walmart.com)
Xerox (www.xerox.com)

These are but a few references. There's others out there that could be chosen from as well.

The options of doing business with other companies are endless. Almost every company offers the commercial account, Net-30 terms and report directly to Dun & Bradstreet. Just be sure to choose companies that will boost your company's credit ratings. Once you have a Dun & Bradstreet score established, credit lines from as far away as you can imagine, will be wanting to capture your company's business.

SHORTCUT TO BUSINESS CREDIT

Now say for some reason you wanna skip all the Dun & Bradstreet logistics, which I highly disapprove. But you need some credit to get your company off the ground, and like in J.G. Wentworth's words, "YOU NEED IT NOW!"

Well I feel obligated to show you a surefire shortcut that can possibly attain you a good amount in unsecured credit lines; and at the same time, boost your company's credit rating, absent a Dun & Bradstreet membership. Here's what you do in the following order:

a. You'll first need to incorporate with your Secretary of State;

b. Next you'll need to secure your EIN number with the IRS;

c. You'll need to secure a business telephone line, which lists your company's telephone number in the directory;

d. You'll need to secure the appropriate business license from your local tax collector's office or at your county courthouse;

e. You'll need to open your corporate accounts (remember, one which is a main one that you use for paying everyone; and the one you use to transfer profits and savings to);

f. The next thing you'll need to do is shop around for all the unsecured credit cards that you can receive, for whatever amount you're approved for.

Most credit card companies will charge you an application or processing fee, but allow the fee to be deducted from whatever credit line you're approved for;

g. Once you obtain all the unsecured credit lines, be smart and use it specifically for the business. Be additionally wise to spend it on the premise that it will generate profitable business income, which produce enough income to pay off the credit lines and their interest.

If the type of field your company operates in is lets say, entertainment, then hell, promote shows as well. What you want is the company to get off the ground, and this is the only money you have at that chance. You have to look at it from the perspective of: if you lose or misuse it, then you'll be homeless and unable to provide for yourself or your family by the time it runs out. This is seriously how you have to take it.

My father once gave me the best investment advice. Till this day I have never heard anyone else mention it. He says son, there's three investments that no one can ever stop from profiting. He says, I can't stop them, you can't stop them, your kids can't stop them, your kids kids can't stop them, and neither could a hundred Generations of your kids. No one can. He goes on to say that they're: The housing Market (never believe that there's ever such a thing as a housing bubble burst), Bail Bonds (because people are always going to jail. And weekends and holidays boom the most), and the final one is funeral homes. There you have it. People will always be born and need somewhere to stay. The police will always put somebody ass in jail, especially when the punishment is unjust. And people will always die.

That always stuck with me and from that point in my life, I aimed to invest in things that was almost certainly risk-proof. So make what you do with the money count;

h. Now once you spend the money, make sure you spend it all at once. This is because if credit card companies are witnessing you unloading credit limit after credit limit, they'll flag you and freeze and or terminate your credit line and account with them, to prevent their company from assumable fraud loss. Those actions taken on your behalf will reflect to the credit Bureaus as being suspicious. So don't unload one credit card today and then another credit card tomorrow, and another credit card the next day after that. Find and price-check everything it takes for the business to run itself, until it starts generating enough income to run on its own. Then purchase all of your necessities at once. This should take longer than 30 to 45 days.

The next moves are smooth, so pay close attention
i. You should make a call to each credit line lender and explain your position of being a new corporation, with an approved unsecured credit line with them.

Inform them that you've maxed out your credit line limit in exchange for business necessities that is guaranteed to have business income pouring in. But that you have one obstacle: It will take no longer than 6 months, and that what you need from them is a 6-month deferred payment plan, with whatever interest they feel is fair to them, for their patience, even if it require that you personally guarantee the loan. **Why not, The money is already spent anyway? What do you have to lose?**

When the credit lender agree is when things gets beautiful. They'll be greedy at the sound of hearing 'selective interest' or 'set interest' and immediately vision dollar signs in their heads. But actually, the dollar signs should be ringing in your heads. Because each month, those credit lenders will have score your company as "PAID-N-FULL" and rate it as "PAID AS AGREED."

Anything other than that would void them of your contract, and your owing them NO NAHN NOTHER RED CENT! Here's why:

Each credit lender have to report a listing each month, on every company loaded in their databases which has a credit debt to them. The listings are calculated on a monthly basis based on the premium amounts dolled out to the Debtors, by the lenders. Well, the lenders can't list a negative, poor or slow-to-pay report on your company because they have agreed to the deferred payment plan, with higher interest rates they normally wouldn't receive. So each month, the lenders must list you as a "GRADE A" paying client, until and unless you haven't paid after the sixth month.

By this time, the company have attracted unlimited unsecured credit line amounts from other credit line lenders, who've been eyeing the ratings and responsibility of your new company. Some of these "eye-ballers" are probably lenders that were afraid to take a chance with loaning the company money at the outset.

By this time, if your company haven't started generating positive income before the 6th month deadline, then your company could utilize the new proposed credit lines and pay back the first credit line lenders with those; and then negotiate a new 6 month deferred payment plan with the new credit line lenders, repeating the process over again. In this way, you'll have an additional 6 months to generate good income for your business.

Now imagine how your company: will look if you secured 100k in unsecured credit on its behalf; had a "PAID-N-FULL" and "PAID AS AGREED" rating, every month; and then an "OBLIGATION FULFILLMENT" at the 6-month marker?

I'll help you with the outcome of that imagination: You'll be on your way to a $250k unsecured credit line. Then next a $500k unsecured credit line. Then 1 Million, and so on.

But like I say, you have to use the money wisely. At least wise enough so that the company could start generating money; and the money is more than enough to pay back the credit line limits, with its interest.

This method, I must say, is very addictive. So don't get besides yourself and establish corporations to repeat this process over and over with ill intentions.

Here are some websites to get you started, while on your hunt for credit cards:

Credit Card.com
www.creditcards.com/business.php

Card Ratings
www.cardratings.com (click on business cards under card reports)

Low Cards
www.lowcards.com/businesscards.asp

Money Search
www.moneysearch.com/creditcards/businesscreditcards.html

Penn Treaty Financial
www.penntreatyfinancial.com

American Express
www.open.com/applybusinessgold

Discover
www.discover.com

Capital One
www.capitalone.com/smallbusiness

Chase
www.chase.com

CHAPTER 9

FIXING YOUR OWN CREDIT & EXCLUDING CREDIT REPAIRERS

FIXING YOUR CREDIT & EXCLUDING CREDIT REPAIRERS

In this Chapter I wanna show you how to fix your personal credit and obtain free credit reports even if the last report you requested were within six months. Why pay credit repairers money to 'so called' fix your credit, when you can do it more efficiently yourself and not pay a dime? And depending on how prompt the credit consumer agency fix your credit record, you may be entitled to certain damages under a lawsuit.

Congress enacted "THE FAIR CONSUMER REPORTING ACT" (FCRA) to Mandate consumer reporting agencies to adopt reasonable procedures for meeting the needs of commerce for consumer credit, personnel, insurance and other information, in a manner which is fair and equitable to the consumer, with regard to the confidentiality, accuracy, relevancy and proper utilisation of such information. 15 U.S.C. §1681(b) This means that Congress enacted certain guidelines for credit agencies to follow as it regarded certain information regarding individuals of the public's credit. Those rules and guidelines established that when a credit report is requested to be corrected, the credit agency has to forward subscribers a "Consumer Dispute Verification" (CDV) form, asking the subscriber to check whether the information they have about that particular consumer matches the information that was docketed in the credit report.

If a subscriber fails to respond or indicates that the account information is incorrect then the credit agency will delete the disputed information, which usually takes no longer than 8 weeks.
Congress specifically set these rules and guidelines out in detail.

Therefore, to guard against the use of inaccurate or arbitrary information in evaluating an individual for credit, insurance, or employment, Congress additionally required that consumer reporting agencies "follow reasonable procedures to assure maximum possible accuracy of the information concerning the individual about whom a credit report relates." 15 U.S.C. §1681(e)(b)

See also 15 U.S.C. §1681(i)(a) wherein Congress established that "when the credit agency receives a complaint, the credit agency must reinvestigate the disputed information that has been found to be inaccurate or unverifiable." When the disputed information is inaccurate or unverifiable then said information MUST be removed; and the credit agency MUST place the individual on notice of such removal; and if requested, provide the individual a new credit report showing that the disputed or unverifiable information has been removed or corrected. This principle is also Governed under 15 U.S.C.; 1681(d) and §1681(i)(d), explaining that, upon reinvestigation and deletion of inaccurate items from a credit report, consumer reporting agencies "SHALL, at the request of the consumer, furnish notification that the item has been deleted....to any person specifically designated by the consumer whom has....within six months prior thereto received a consumer report....which contained the deleted or disputed information."

Because the burden rests however, with the consumer to request the updated report, the act also required that "the consumer reporting agency SHALL clearly and conspicuously disclose to the consumer his rights to make such a request." Such disclosures shall be made at or prior to the time the information is deleted or the consumer's statement regarding the disputed information is received.

A consumer reporting agency that negligently fails to comply with FCRA's requirements is liable for actual damages, costs and reasonable attorney fees. 15 U.S.C. §1681(o)

And under such violations, 'willful noncompliance' renders a consumer reporting agency additionally liable for punitive damages. 15 U.S.C. §1681(n)

An example of 'negligence' is when the credit agency allows inaccurate or unverifidble information back onto a credit report after it had been deleted.

see Morris V. Credit Bureau of Cincinnati, Inc., 563 F.supp. 962, 968 (S.D. Ohio 1983). Other courts have made or upheld similar awards. see Collins V. Retail Credit Co., 410 F.supp. 924, 936 (E.D. Mich. 1976); Bryant V. TRW, Inc., 486 F.Supp. 1234, 1242-43 (E.D. Mich. 1980); Millstone V. O'Hanlon Reports, Inc., 528 F.2d 829, 834-35 (8th Cir. 1976); and Pinner V. Schmidt, 805 F.2d 1258, 1263 (5th Cir. 1986).

I have enclosed two drafted letters that will enable you to fix your own credit and receive a new credit report with the updated inaccurate or unverifiable information removed.

The reason I'm almost certain that your credit will be fixed is because most subscribers that submit negative or unverifiable information to credit agencies do so via purchasing debt. The debt however, has to be debt that you yourself accumulated with the subscriber whom is reporting to the credit agency. There can be no negative or unverifiable information submitted by a third party which did not initially own the debt. What this means is that if the debt you owed was purchased by a third party, then that negative information would be removed from your credit report because now the debt becomes unverifiable. And almost all debts submitted to credit bureaus are submitted by third party purchasers looking to cash in on whatever they can retrieve from the debt, with the exception of child support.

So copy and fill out the credit form on the next page and mail it out to the address listed thereon. Remember to check all three circles so that you'd receive a credit report from all three agencies. If you have already made an inquiry within the last three months then disregard the form and follow the following instructions.

a. retype and mail out the first letter (once fully filled out). Send one to every credit agency.

b. If you do not receive anything from the credit agency within six weeks, then mail out the 2nd letter.

The key to all of this is that you have to certify both letters to the credit agencies.

c. If you do not receive anything within another six week period then take the credit bureau to court. You'll win the lawsuit hands down and receive damages for mental anguish, libel, willful noncompliance, neglect, embarrassment, humiliation and attorney fees.

Keep a copy of the two letters for your personal records, along with copies of your certified receipts; and you are guaranteed to win the case by settlement.

But from experience, the credit agencies will promptly reply and investigate your claims. If the claims are not verifiable then they will remove the negative and or inaccurate information from your credit report. And each one of them will provide you a new report showing that the negative and or unverifiable information have been removed. **Just submit a new credit report inquiry in about six months later to confirm that the information don't reappear.**

On the following page is the addresses to all three credit Bureaus. Remember, send a letter to each one of them.

EQUIFAX
P.O. Box 105314
Atlanta, Georgia
30348

EXPERIAN
NCAC
P.O. Box 9701
Allen, Texas
75013

TRANSUNION
P.O. Box 1000
Chester, Pennsylvania
19022-1000

Annual Credit Report Request Form

You have the right to get a free copy of your credit file disclosure, commonly called a credit report, once every 12 months, from each of the nationwide consumer credit reporting companies, Equifax, Experian and TransUnion. For instant access to your free credit report, visit www.annualcreditreport.com.

For more information on obtaining your free credit report, visit www.annualcreditreport.com or call 877-322-8228. Use this form if you prefer to write to request your credit report from any, or all, of the nationwide consumer credit reporting companies. The following information is required to process your request. Omission of any information may delay your request.

Please use a Black or Blue pen and write your responses in PRINTED CAPITAL LETTERS without touching the sides of the boxes like the examples listed below:

A B C D E F G H I J K L M N O P Q R S T U V W X Y Z 0 1 2 3 4 5 6 7 8 9

Social Security Number:

Date of Birth Month / Day / Year

Fold Here — Fold Here

First name — **M.I**

Last Name — JR, SR, III, etc.

Current Mailing Address:

House Number — Street name

Apartment Number / Private Mailbox — For Puerto Rico Only: Print Urbanization Name

City — State — Zipcode

Previous Mailing Address (complete only if at current mailing address for less than two

House Number — Street name

Fold Here — Fold Here

Apartment Number / Private Mailbox — For Puerto Rico Only: Print Urbanization Name

City — State — Zipcode

Shade Circle Like This ➔ ●
Not Like This ➔ ⊗ ✓

I want a credit report from (shade each that you would like to receive):
○ Equifax
○ Experian
○ TransUnion

○ Shade here if, for security reasons, you want your credit report to include no more than the last four digits of your Social Security Number.

If additional information is needed to process your request, the consumer credit reporting company will contact you by mail. Your request will be processed within 15 days of receipt and then mailed to you.

Copyright 2004, Central Source LLC 31238

Once complete, fold (do not staple or tape), place into a #10 envelope, affix required postage and mail to:
Annual Credit Report Request Service P.O. Box 105281 Atlanta, GA 30348-5281.

date:

Certified Receipt No. _____

Full Name
D.O.B.
Social Security Number
Address
City, State and Zip Code

In re: Credit Discrepancies

Dear Credit Agency Processor,

I am _____, with a date of birth of _____, a social security number of_____ and an address of _____, City of _____, State of _____, Zip Code _____.
I have reviewed my credit report and found that all of the current entries are **"INCORRECT."**
I am hereby making a complaint regarding the inaccurate information contained thereon; and am respectfully requesting that you forward a "Consumer Dispute Verification Form (CDV)" to all of the 'claimed subscribers' and remove ALL accounts containing "negative" credit information.
It is further respectfully requested that you furnish me notification that "ALL" negative items have been deleted after a thorough investigation into this matter.
I am pursuing this matter in accordance with the laws of CONGRESS pursuant to "THE FAIR CREDIT REPORTING ACT" of §1681; and I expect a prompt investigation and correction of said matter.

Sincerely,

date:

Certified Receipt No. _____

Full Name
D.O.B.
Social Security Number
Address
City, State and Zip Code

In re: Credit Discrepancies

Dear Credit Agency Processor,

My recently respectful request has not been complied with in accordance with "THE FAIR CREDIT REPORTING ACT" of §1681; and I'm placing this credit agency on notice that it could be acting willfully and negligently, and subject to a suit for actual damages, mental anguish, punitive damages and attorney fees, by not deleting unverifiable and or inaccurate information pursuant to Section §1681(i) (d); §1681(o); and <u>Pinner V. Schmidt</u>, 805 F.2d 1258, 1263 (5th cir. 1986) cert. denied, 483 U.S. 1022; [987 F.2d 294] 107 S.CT. 3267, 97 L.ed 2d 766 (1987). Congress enacted the FCRA to require consumer reporting agencies to adopt reasonable procedures for meeting the needs of commerce for consumer credit and other information, in a manner which is fair and equitable to the consumer, with regards to the confidentiality, accuracy, relevancy and proper utilization of such information. see 15 U.S.C. §1681(b).

To guard against the use of inaccurate or arbitrary information in evaluating an individual credit, Congress further Mandated that consumer reporting agencies follow reasonable procedures to assure maximum possible accuracy of the information concerning the individual about whom a credit report relates. Willful noncompliance renders a consumer reporting agency additionally liable for punitive damages. When it receives the complaint, a consumer reporting agency must investigate the disputed information and "promptly" delete the credit information that has been found to be inaccurate or verifiable. see 15 U.S.C. §1681(i) (a). At the request of the consumer, the credit reporting agency must furnish the new consumer report which contain deleted or disputed information. 15 U.S.C. §1681(i)(d).

Would you please comply with the intent of Congress and grant the request set out in my initial correspondence dated _____.

Sincerely,

UNIFORM COMMERCIAL CODE (UCC)

Before we reach the "Securing Business Loans" chapter, its very important you know, understand and familiarize yourself with how banks operate and the Uniform Commercial Code (UCC).

The Uniform Commercial Code is prepared under the joint sponsorship of the American Law Institute and the National Conference of Commissioners on uniform state laws; and which are in effect in most states of the United States at the time of enactment.

Its Governed by the Uniform Code Counsel but its operations and functioning extends far beyond.

One of its reasons of establishment was for its creation of banking laws and governance of its codes during transactions in commercial and interstate dealings.

Why is any of this relevant? Because banks operate on another level of functioning than what the public knows and believe. They seem to have created and conducted a "MATRIX" operation with floating numbers that is stored in a private database for a number of unknown odd reasons. Those numbers breakdown every known detail regarding a person or product; and which then creates a unified control which manipulates human life through robotic and electronic methods as if humans themselves are instead virtual beings, just like in the movie.

Think about the metric system, which is where the name 'Matrix' derive. Now ponder on the fact of all the numbers that you have encountered throughout your life: birth certificate numbers, death certificate numbers, credit card numbers, social security numbers, EIN numbers, driver's license numbers, date of birth numbers, identification numbers, day month and year numbers, bank account numbers, employee numbers, combination numbers, time of day numbers, import/export numbers, vin numbers, tag numbers, tracking numbers, routing numbers, transaction numbers, stock certificate numbers, ISBN's and other bar code numbers and on and on.

Everything is identified by numbers, anything that you can think of. Paint number, part number, pin number, password, passcode, etc. Its an implemented comprehensive system that has come too far to be unraveled; and its Governed by codes, regulations and regulators under Uniform Commercial Code (UCC). Sounding like Government conspiracy shit?....It probably is.

But don't grow grey hair overnight on what I just pointed out because I'm about to show you how UCC could be utilized to your advantage in the financial aspect.

I stated to you earlier on the importance of copyrighting and trademarking your company's name, image and content; along with the importance of obtaining the domain name and other material that you have associated with it.

The reason for telling you that is because all of these things holds tremendous value. Its a company's asset. And owning it in your personal capacity is a win win situation for you. So what you must do at the outset is buy everything in your personal name **(not your company's name).**

Things like your copyrights, trademarks, domain name(s), logo design, visa prepaid credit card, UPS Suite address and anything else that you can tie to the company (meaning ideas, drafts, sketches, notes, patterns, drawings, etc.). I'll explain how it'll value your company in a minute, but meanwhile, make sure you take care of this. Don't worry yet about incorporating or opening any accounts as of yet, but if you have, don't do anything other than that because I want you to know more about UCC first, and how beneficial it could be.

The fundamental principle of UCC is that it affords you a lien ownership that can be used as collateral towards a loan to upstart your company, or upgrade your personal life to appear more professional while running your company.

Don't expect anyone to be familiar with UCC because no one wants anyone to provide a floodgate to the public regarding its benefits. Its used by a quiet society whom will stop at nothing to keep those unfamiliar with it, from knowing about it. And thus, banking officials don't expect for certain groups of people to understand how it operates. But UCC is simple, and yet at the same time, fascinating. If utilized correctly, it could reap you lucrative rewards from loan officers and investors alike. Below is two UCC forms that you'll most likely ever need. They're both unique in their own way, but wonderful when used synonymously. I'll explain further what they do and how they work in detail so that you'll be more educated on the subject. Then I'll cut strait to the chase in the "Securing Business Loans" section and show you exactly how to use them.

The first form is called a UCC-1 Form. **I have supplied the form closest to a universal use. If the State of Florida is not your state then write to your Secretary of State at the address listed in the "Corporation" section and request their UCC-1 Financial Statement.**

The form must be completely legible, in either typed or laser print. The correct Debtor's name is crucial, as well as the Secured Party's. Mistakes may have important legal and civil consequences. Additionally, the Secretary of State's filing office cannot render legal advice.

Now, as I stated, lets take a look at the UCC-1 Form, which is known as a UCC-1 Financial Statement.

It is first most important not to insert anything in the open space in the upper portion of the form because it is reserved for the filing office's use only.

I'll walk you through the remainder of the form by the alphabetical order of the alphabets and or numbers:

STATE OF FLORIDA UNIFORM COMMERCIAL CODE FINANCING STATEMENT FORM

A. NAME & DAYTIME PHONE NUMBER OF CONTACT PERSON

B. SEND ACKNOWLEDGEMENT TO:
Name
Address
Address
City/State/Zip

THE ABOVE SPACE IS FOR FILING OFFICE USE ONLY

1. DEBTOR'S EXACT FULL LEGAL NAME – INSERT ONLY **ONE** DEBTOR NAME **(1a OR 1b)** – Do Not Abbreviate or Combine Names

1.a ORGANIZATION'S NAME				
1.b INDIVIDUAL'S LAST NAME		FIRST NAME	MIDDLE NAME	SUFFIX
1.c MAILING ADDRESS Line One		This space not available.		
MAILING ADDRESS Line Two	CITY	STATE	POSTAL CODE	COUNTRY
1.d TAX ID#	REQUIRED ADD'L INFO RE: ORGANIZATION DEBTOR	1.e TYPE OF ORGANIZATION	1.f JURISDICTION OF ORGANIZATION	1.g ORGANIZATIONAL ID# NONE

2. ADDITIONAL DEBTOR'S EXACT FULL LEGAL NAME – INSERT ONLY **ONE** DEBTOR NAME **(2a OR 2b)** – Do Not Abbreviate or Combine Names

2.a ORGANIZATION'S NAME				
2.b INDIVIDUAL'S LAST NAME		FIRST NAME	MIDDLE NAME	SUFFIX
2.c MAILING ADDRESS Line One		This space not available.		
MAILING ADDRESS Line Two	CITY	STATE	POSTAL CODE	COUNTRY
2.d TAX ID#	REQUIRED ADD'L INFO RE: ORGANIZATION DEBTOR	2.e TYPE OF ORGANIZATION	2.f JURISDICTION OF ORGANIZATION	2.g ORGANIZATIONAL ID#

3. SECURED PARTY'S NAME (or NAME of TOTAL ASSIGNEE of ASSIGNOR S/P) – INSERT ONLY **ONE** SECURED PARTY **(3a OR 3b)**

3.a ORGANIZATION'S NAME				
3.b INDIVIDUAL'S LAST NAME		FIRST NAME	MIDDLE NAME	SUFFIX
3.c MAILING ADDRESS Line One		This space not available.		
MAILING ADDRESS Line Two	CITY	STATE	POSTAL CODE	COUNTRY
3.d TAX ID#	REQUIRED ADD'L INFO RE: ORGANIZATION DEBTOR	3.e TYPE OF ORGANIZATION	3.f JURISDICTION OF ORGANIZATION	3.g ORGANIZATIONAL ID#

4. This **FINANCING STATEMENT** covers the following collateral:

5. ALTERNATE DESIGNATION (if applicable)
☐ LESSEE/LESSOR ☐ CONSIGNEE/CONSIGNOR ☐ BAILEE/BAILOR
☐ AG. LIEN ☐ NON-UCC FILING ☐ SELLER/BUYER

6. Florida DOCUMENTARY STAMP TAX – YOU ARE REQUIRED TO CHECK **EXACTLY ONE** BOX
☐ All documentary stamps due and payable or to become due and payable pursuant to s. 201.22 F.S., have been paid.
☐ Florida Documentary Stamp Tax is not required.

7. OPTIONAL FILER REFERENCE DATA

STANDARD FORM - FORM UCC-1 (REV.01/2009)   Filing Office Copy   Approved by the Secretary of State, State of Florida

STATE OF FLORIDA UNIFORM COMMERCIAL CODE FINANCING STATEMENT AMENDMENT FORM

A. NAME & DAYTIME PHONE NUMBER OF CONTACT PERSON

B. SEND ACKNOWLEDGEMENT TO:
Name
Address
Address
City/State/Zip

THE ABOVE SPACE IS FOR FILING OFFICE USE ONLY

1a. INITIAL FINANCING STATEMENT FILE #

1b. ☐ This FINANCING STATEMENT AMENDMENT is to be filed [for record] (or recorded) in the REAL ESTATE RECORDS.

2. CURRENT RECORD INFORMATION – DEBTOR NAME – INSERT ONLY ONE DEBTOR NAME (2a OR 2b)

2.a ORGANIZATION'S NAME			
2.b INDIVIDUAL'S LAST NAME	FIRST NAME	MIDDLE NAME	SUFFIX

3. CURRENT RECORD INFORMATION – SECURED PARTY NAME – INSERT ONLY ONE SECURED PARTY NAME (3a OR 3b)

3.a ORGANIZATION'S NAME			
3.b INDIVIDUAL'S LAST NAME	FIRST NAME	MIDDLE NAME	SUFFIX

4. ☐ **TERMINATION:** Effectiveness of the Financing Statement identified above is terminated with respect to security interest(s) of the Secured Party authorizing this Termination Statement.

5. ☐ **CONTINUATION:** Effectiveness of the Financing Statement identified above with respect to security interest(s) of the Secured Party authorizing this Continuation Statement is continued for the additional period provided by applicable law.

6. ☐ **ASSIGNMENT (full or partial):** Give name of assignee in item 9a or 9b and address of assignee in item 9c; and also give name of assignor in item 11.

7. ☐ **AMENDMENT (PARTY INFORMATION):** This Amendment affects ☐ Debtor or ☐ Secured Party of record. Check only one of these two boxes.
Also check one of the following three boxes and provide appropriate information in items 8 and/or 9.

☐ CHANGE name and/or address: Give current record name in item 8a or 8b; Also give new name (if name change) in item 9a or 9b and/or new address (if address change) in item 9c.

☐ DELETE name: Give record name to be deleted in item 8a or 8b.

☐ ADD name: Complete item 9a or 9b, and 9c; also complete items 9d-9g (if applicable)..

8. CURRENT RECORD INFORMATION – INSERT ONLY ONE NAME (8a OR 8b) – Do Not Abbreviate or Combine Names

8.a ORGANIZATION'S NAME			
8.b INDIVIDUAL'S LAST NAME	FIRST NAME	MIDDLE NAME	SUFFIX

9. CHANGED (NEW) OR ADDED INFORMATION: – INSERT ONLY ONE NAME (9a OR 9b) – Do Not Abbreviate or Combine Names

9.a ORGANIZATION'S NAME				
9.b INDIVIDUAL'S LAST NAME		FIRST NAME	MIDDLE NAME	SUFFIX
9.c MAILING ADDRESS Line One		This space not available.		
MAILING ADDRESS Line Two	CITY	STATE	POSTAL CODE	COUNTRY
9.d TAX ID#	REQUIRED ADD'L INFO RE: ORGANIZATION DEBTOR	9.e TYPE OF ORGANIZATION	9.f JURISDICTION OF ORGANIZATION	9.g ORGANIZATIONAL ID#

10. AMENDMENT (COLLATERAL CHANGE): check only one box.
Describe collateral ☐ deleted or ☐ added, or give entire ☐ restated collateral description, ☐ or describe assigned. collateral

11. NAME OF SECURED PARTY OF RECORD AUTHORIZING THIS AMENDMENT (name of assignor, if this is an Assignment). If this is an Amendment authorized by a Debtor, which adds collateral or adds the authorizing Debtor, or if this is a Termination authorized by a Debtor, check here ☐ and enter name of DEBTOR authorizing this Amendment.

11.a ORGANIZATION'S NAME			
11.b INDIVIDUAL'S LAST NAME	FIRST NAME	MIDDLE NAME	SUFFIX

12. OPTIONAL FILER REFERENCE DATA

STANDARD FORM - FORM UCC - 3 (REV.01/2009)   Filling office copy   Approved by the Secretary if State, State if Florida

FAMILIARIZING YOURSELF WITH UCC

A. To assist filing offices that might wish to communicate with the filer hereof (yourself), then provide the optional information in this item;

B. Complete item B if you want an acknowledgement sent to you. Most times, this will be a packet verifying your filings on record;

1. This section consists of Debtor's exact full name, which must not be combined and or abbreviated;

1a, Organization Same.
This is always the Debtor in its entity name, having a legal identity separate from its owner.
The 'organization name' is usually the corporation, LLC, General or Limited Partnership's full name with its suffixes (for example, names that end with Inc., Corp., Co., LLC, L.L.C., Ltd., etc.);

1b, Individual's full and Last Name.
This means a natural person, without the prefixes of Mr., Mrs., Ms., etc. This person is usually the Chairman of the Organization above. The suffix section should only indicate if the identity is a Jr., Sr., III, etc.;

1c. An address is always required for the Debtor's name in "1a" only. Any personal addresses should be inserted in the "acknowledgement" section in Block B at the top of the form;

1d, Tax i.d. Number.
This is reserved for Debtor's EIN Number;

1e, Type of Organization.
The type of Organization should be entered here. That is, C Corporation, LLC, etc.;

If, Jurisdiction of Organization.
Jurisdiction would be listed as the State in which Debtor was established in;

1g, Organizational i.d. Number.
This is different from the EIN Number listed in "Id." This is the number assigned to the organization by the Secretary of State;

Since the next section doesn't apply, we'll skip it (Section 2) in its entirety and move on to Section 3, which is "Secured Party's Name." **Remember however, that Debtor is the one whom OWES the debt.**

3a, Organization's Name.
Fill this block out if Secured Party is another corporation, LLC, etc.;

3b, Individual's Name.
Fill this section out with the Secured Party's personal information. **The Secured Party is the one whom a debt is owed to;**

3c Mailing Address.
Fill these sections in with the Secured Party's full mailing address;

4. Financial Statement.
Don't worry about this section, I'll help you with the insertions you need when we get to the second chapter from this one;

5. Alternative Designation.
Don't concern yourself with this section;

6. Documentary Stamp Tax.
Check the first box;

7. Optional Filer Reference Data.
This is optional and irrelevant, so don't concern yourself about it either.

When everything is complete, there's a Promissory Note and a UCC-1 Security Agreement (which we'll discuss later), that is **ALWAYS** attached and submitted with the filing. Never submit just the UCC-1 Financial Statement. **YOU CANNOT PERFECT A LIEN WITHOUT THE BOTH OF THEM.** Hope I drilled that into your head.

Now lets take a look at the next 'Most Valuable' UCC form. Its called a UCC-3 and you'll only need it in two situations. One of those situations are if you have a Promissory Note with a life expectancy exceeding 5 years, and the other is if you have to pledge or sell your Promissory Note to another.

In the first scenario, if you have a Promissory Note that has to be paid out to you over a five year period, then you have to file the UCC-3 form, which is basically known as a "MAINTENANCE," prior to the last day of the fifth year. It is of PARAMOUNT importance that you not allow the Promissory Note to exceed the last day of the fifth year. If that happens then your debt has collapsed by technicality of your own fault and you won't be able to collect on your payout any further. **SO BE SURE TO STAY ON YOUR GAME WITH THIS ONE,** which means that if you hold a Promissory Note against someone that matures over a five year period, then you HAVE TO renew the Note at least on the last day prior to the fifth year. And this is done by using the UCC-3 form.

In the second scenario, you will need to file the UCC-3 form if you have to use the Promissory Note for collateral on a loan from a bank, investor, lender or financial backer. In this case they may want you to pledge, or even turn over your Promissory Note to them as security, in exchange for their loan. This is called an '**assignment.**' The remainder reasons for using the UCC-3 is unimportant to this book.

Now that I have covered the two most important points after the Promissory Note is issued and the UCC-1 Security Agreement is filed, I believe its safe to continue ahead and explain the content on the UCC-3 form, and how the form is filled out.

First, the same block in **"A. and B. above all"** is to be filled out the same as it was in the UCC-1 Financial Statement form;

1a, Initial Financing Statement File #.
This is the file Number that was assigned to you by your Secretary of State when it Filed and Registered your UCC-1 Financial Statement;

1b, Financing Statement Amendment.
Disregard this section because we're not referencing real estate nor its records;

2, Current Record Information – Debtor Same.
2a, Organization's Name.

This section is reserved for the same Organization's name whom you listed as the Debtor on the UCC-1 Financial Statement form;

2b, Individual's Full Name.
This section is reserved for the same Full Name of the identity of the person that was listed in the UCC-1 Financial Statement Form, if said person **was not** a company, corporation, etc.;

3, Current Record Information – Secured Party.
3a, Organization Name.
List the Name of the Organisation that you listed in the UCC-1 Financial Statement. **Remember,** this regards the Secured Party;

3b, Individual's Full Name.
This would be the same Secured Party individual as you listed in the UCC-1 Financial Statement, if Secured Party was not a Corporation, LLC, etc.;

4, Termination; 5, Continuation; or 6, Assignment.
Check one of these boxes;

7, Amendment.
If this is an 'Amendment' then check the first box.

AN Amendment is when you have a situation that was either left off the initial UCC-1 Financial Statement or is now adding to this Form.

Such an amendment could also result if you are selling your Promissory Note to another company or individual. In some cases, it can also be utilized if you are pledging your Promissory Note as collateral on a personal loan.

HOWEVER, if this is an amendment and it affects debtor (the one whom owes), then check the second box on the top of this section. If it affects the Secured Party then check the third box on the top in this section.

FAMILIARIZING YOURSELF WITH UCC

If the amendment is in the best interest of the Debtor then it would affect the Secured Party. If it is in the best interest of the Secured Party then it would affect the debtor.

If the amendment is simply to change a name then check the first box in this section on the bottom; and fill in **"8a. and or 8b."**

If the amendment is simply to change an address then check the same box and fill in sections **9a, 9b, 9e, 9d, 9e, 9f and 9g.**

HOWEVER, if the amendment of the name and or address change affects either the Debtor or the Secured Party, then the box must demonstrate which one it applies to (that is, Debtor, which is the top second box in this section), or Secured Party (which is the top third box in this section).

If the amendment is to DELETE a name or address then you must include in Section **8 and 9** the full names and addresses that is requested to be DELETED.

If the amendment is to **ADD** a name or address, then you must include in section **8 and 9** the full names and addresses that is requested to be ADDED;

10, Amendment (Collateral Change).
If the amendment is to DELETE collateral that was listed in the UCC-1 Financial Statement, then check the first box in this section and describe in detail the collateral that is being DELETED from the UCC-1 Financial Statement.

If the amendment is to ADD additional property other than what was stated in the first UCC-1 Financial Statement, then check the second box and describe in detail the collateral or property that is to be ADDED to the UCC-1 Financial Statement.

If the amendment is to 'state in exact detail or specify the exact property that was described in the UCC-1 Financial Statement' then check the third box and clarify the collateral or property that was listed in the first UCC-1 Financial Statement.

If the amendment is to assign the property listed in the first UCC-1 Financial Statement to someone else, then cheek the last box in this section and reaffirm the property that was listed in the UCC-1 Financial Statement;

11, Name of Secured Party Authorizing This Amendment.
If this is an assignment then enter the name of the Secured Party that was listed in the UCC-1 Financial Statement. But add 'assignor' next to the Organization name (if the Secured Party in the UCC-1 Financial Statement is an Organization). If this was an amendment authorized by Debtor, which ADDS collateral **or** ADDS an authorizing Debtor; or if this amendment is an termination authorized by Debtor, then check the box in 11. And add the name of Debtor. **Be sure to** ADD 'Debtor' by the name filled out in section **11a. and 11b.** Remember that sections 4, 5 and 6 are self explanatory.

Well, I hope I enlightened you somewhat on the subject matter of UCC and how the two most important forms of it are used. I don't expect you to know all there is about it and all the many ways it could be used and or useful in securing loans. In such regard, you'll have to do your own studying and research on the matter. My reasons of wanting you to be familiar with it is because you will have to know of it when securing business loans, and I wanted you to be aware of its powers. However, these powers are even ways away from utilizing UCC of reaching its highest potential.

CHAPTER 11
ASSIGNING YOUR BUSINESS A SOLID ASSET

FORMING SOLID BUSINESS ASSETS

Remember the story that I told you about, regarding the three businesses which my father said would never stop producing lucrative income? Well guess what, I pondered that for some time and came upon the idea of something even more power than those. In fact, what I discovered was what drove those businesses to the brink of ever evolving success. With this in mind I would like to quiz you but for a second to see what type of level you're on. Can you tell me what business exist today that runs the world?

If you said Insurance then you should be able to take this book and do some fascinating numbers with it.

But you're right, Insurance here is the answer. Everything is fueled by Insurance. Lets check: Car insurance, house insurance, boat insurance, life insurance, flood insurance, fire insurance, homeowners insurance, dental insurance, medical insurance, motorcycle insurance, rv insurance, property insurance, ass insurance, breast insurance, etc. Get my drift?

Nothing gets produced without it being insured and or an insurance underwriter insuring it. To put this in better perspective, allow me to point out that you are walking (or rolling if you're handicapped) money. Many people live in our society and need money such as loans and etc. but cannot approach a bank, lender or financial institution because they don't have any collateral. I'm interested to know who was it that led them to believe this lie. Because if it was so then why is there insurance agents and the likes soliciting to sell them insurance?

Since this book is about cutting strait to the chase, I won't go into too much detail about the magnificence of insurance. I'm here to show you how to use it to give your business a solid asset.

The first thing you wanna do when you finish incorporating and opening your accounts is purchase a million dollar life insurance policy on yourself. Since you're the only real employee (because everyone else is not actually employees, they're independent contractors).

The younger you are the cheaper the policy premiums. Your down payment seals your policy, and it thus, automatically becomes a solid asset. Instantly, your company becomes worth a million dollars, as secured by your policy. If there were other employees working for you (not independent contractors), then you can also secure million dollar policies out on them as well. **However, you must be careful in this area to know that you just can't run around taking insurance policies out on people. There's a such crime called a STOLI Scheme that calls for lengthy prison sentences. You can only secure insurance policies on you and your employees.**

Securing the policies are good investments and require premium payments to be paid annually. So if you had enough money to place down on your insurance policy then you provide your company an instant worth. If a loan is now needed then you have the necessary collateral to secure it.

Now what you can do is perfect the insurance policy with a partial of the loan. For example. If you have a million dollar insurance policy on yourself, which made the company the Beneficiary, and you needed a loan of say 200k. You would advise the bank that you plan on using $50k of that money to purchase a CD (certificate of Deposit) drawing at least 5% annual; using the interest fees to pay the insurance premiums direct deposit. In this way, the insurance policy will never become upset.

Well, say something unfortunate happens to where you can't pay the bank back their loan with interest. Well there's no problem here, the Certificate of Deposit is handed over to the bank and the bank waits on you to expire.

You see, the insurance policy Guaranteed them their money in any event. But now, say you abide by your loan agreement and pay the bank back their loan with interest? awwwww, that's beautiful, the sky is the limit afterwards regarding your responsibility. And the insurance policy's ownership revert back to you and the $50k Certificate of Deposit now becomes yours as well, including its annual interests.

But don't yet think about obtaining loans in this manner. I have a better surefire way that you can obtain them in the next Chapter. What I wanted to do here was give you some insight on insurance policies and how to make them work for your company, giving it an automatic worth to other businesses, banks, lenders, financial backers and etc.

Picture owning a company that owns two million dollars in insurance policies and no debt. Who wouldn't approve it for a loan of say $750k?

Well they understand that $50k will be placed in a CD drawing at least 5% annual interest fees, being paid direct deposit to the insurance premiums, and a portion of the $700k will be paid back to them in monthly payments; and the rest wouldn't matter if you were able to pay them or not because they have two million dollars in which to receive the remainder of their money with interest from, should you die before they're paid. And its highly likely that they'll approve you another loan covering the remainder of what's left out of the two million dollars.

Win win situation for you because if things don't turn out like you wish and or plan, then you just simply create another corporation and repeat the same process. **That's right, there's no limit on the insurance policies that you can obtain. So no law is broken.**

Now, lets move on to "Securing Business Loans."

SECURING A BUSINESS LOAN

I've given you the methods of how companies are scored and rated, I've also given you some insight on securing your company an automatic solid asset, to which could be used as collateral against a loan; and if you were paying any serious attention, securing a business loan should be like taking the pacifier from an infant's mouth. But there's also other secrets that you shouldn't expect anyone in-the-know to inform you about. The way they look at it, the less people know then the more money for them (and whom they decide to share it with).

In this Chapter, I'm getting strait to the point and I need your undivided attention....Hella Money depends on it.

Follow these steps in the chronical order and pick your money up when you get through (that's as ebonics as I can give it to you.)

a. BEFORE ANYTHING, You have to keep **EVERY** receipt;
b. Order a prepaid Visa Credit Card in your personal name and load it with the amount of $3,500 Dollars;
c. Secure your Domain Name(s) with the credit card;
d. Secure the copyrights to that name with the Library of Congress. Use the credit card for the Registration fee;
e. Secure a State trademark or Service Mark for the name of your domain name. Use the credit card also;
f. Secure Your logo design for your copyrighted Name;
g. Secure a UPS box (with a Suite address) from any UPS Store. As of this writing, the price was $45 dollars for 90 days. Secure 1-year's worth under Your copyrighted name;

h. Secure Your United States Trademark from the USPTO (United States Patent and trademark Office);

i. Hire an attorney service to be your incorporator and file your Articles of Incorporation in Your Copyrighted name.

These attorney services (like www.legalzoom.com, www.amerilawyer.com, www.incorporate.com, etc.) also secure other necessary documents on behalf of a company, like the company's Federal Tax i.d. Number, sales tax no., Service Agreements, Sub Chapter 'S' tax status, 1244 LLC Membership interest, Home Office Equipment Lease, Motor Vehicle Lease, Indemnification Agreement and Covenant not to sue, Unemployment Tax Account Number, Employee Benefits and Policies, Employee Agreements, Independent Contractor Agreement, Operating Agreement, General Counsel and Registered Agent Services and etc.;

j. Its very important that the Attorney or Incorporation service list a Non Convicted Felon as the Incorporation's President. This can be a spouse, companion, sibling or other relative. Also be sure to list yourself as an Officer;

NOW, BE SURE TO DO THE FOLLOWING BEFORE YOU FILE YOUR FIRST ANNUAL MINUTES:

k. Now print and fill out the attached contract selling everything in Your personal name to the Corporation (b-h), for the price of one million dollars payable on first demand, and 75,000 shares;

NOW ALLOW THE ATTORNEY TO PREPARE THE CORPORATION'S FIRST ANNUAL MEETING, DOCUMENTING THE TRANSACTION.

l. Direct the president to obtain the necessary business license and permits from Your county's tax collector's office or Your county courthouse;

m. Direct the President to take the 'Bank Resolution' herein, to the biggest Bank in your city and open a corporate Checkings and Savings Account in the company's name.

Open both accounts using a fee of $250 Dollars for each account;

n. While Securing the Checkings and Savings Account the President is directed to execute the Promissory Note before the Banking Official, which is called "AVAL" which means that the banking official will witness the execution of the Promissory Note (followed after the contract selling the intellectual and other property to the corporation), and Stamp the note with the Bank's Medallion;

o. The President shall then shop around (via www.selectquote.com and or at the Insurance Information Institute at www.iii.org) and obtain two insurance policies in the amount of one million dollars each ($1,000,000);

p. You will then secure a $25.00 Dollar U.S. Postal Money Order and purchase a 9x12 manilla envelope.

Deface the envelope with the words "**PLEASE DO NOT BEND**" Then address the envelope to:
Your Secretary or Department of State
"APOSTILLE DIVISION"
City, State and Zip Code
Take the attached first letter following the Promissory Note and place it inside of the Manilla envelope, along with the share Certificate and U.S. Postal Money Order.
Then take down to Your nearest Post Office and mail out by Certified Mail.

q. When the Promissory Note, Share Certificate and its accompanying documents arrive back to you, then take all of those documents, along with the UCC-1 Financial Statement UCC-1 Security Agreement and sort them in the following order:

1. place the UCC-1 Financing statement first;
2. place the UCC-1 Security Agreement second;
3. place the Share Certificate third;
4. place the Promissory Note fourth;

Now hand deliver all of these documents down to your County Clerk Office, in the probate division. Be sure to depart with the originals.

Now Comes The Good Part
Securing a loan at this point should be simple. There are a variety of ways to secure a loan, specifically when U have secured every other stage that was

addressed. One way to secure a loan could be to fund the company's operations. This is a good one due to the fact that banks, investors, and or other financial institutions will want the shares and Promissory note held in escrow, or liend against with the option to reissue the shares and Promissory note to them. At most times they themselves would attempt at perfecting the same Security Agreement as you have perfected against your company. Fear not though, you have the necessary resources to meet this objective. The overall plan is to secure the loan with ease. After all, you hold a lien in a million dollar Promissory note, payable on first demand, in addition to 750,000 of its company shares; and the company has assets of a million dollars, according to the million dollar policy it owns on you; and have no other debts.

The only key factor amongst this all, is to establish a corporation that could make a bank, lender, financial institution or other, its returned loan with interest; and at the same time, that will allow you to make a good living while making the corporation your career.

There are of course, other avenues to secure business loans through, which alot of people are not familiar with. They are as listed below. These loans allow promissory notes and security agreements to be used as collateral, along with the property purchased with the funds:

MICRO LOAN

A micro loan is a loan approved for up to $100,000. Its last known interest rate was 6.53%

7a LOAN

This loan provides for a loan up to 2 million dollars. 75% of it is guaranteed by the Small Business Administration (SBA). 85% is guaranteed by the SBA if the loan is less than $150,000.

SBA EXPRESS LOAN

This loan is for up to $350,000 and 50% of it is guaranteed by the SBA

For more on these loan programs, visit:

www.sba.gov/services/financialassistance/7alenderprograms/sbaexpress/index.html

date:

Your Name
Address
City, State and Zip Code

Certified Receipt No. _____

To Your Secretary or Department of State
"APOSTILLE DIVISION"
City, State and Zip Code

In re: Apostille Certification

Dear Staff,

Enclosed is a U.S. Postal Money Order in the amount of twenty-five ($25.00) dollars.

Also enclosed are a Original Promissory Note and a Share Certificate. A portion of the funds are to be used for "Apostille Certification." As it regards additional funds, please use for next-day air service mailed back to me. Your assistance in this matter is gratefully appreciated.

Sincerely,

date:

Your Name
Address
City, State and Zip Code

Certified Receipt No. _____

To Your Secretary or Department of State
"Records and Registration" Division
City, State and Zip Code

In re: Records and Registration

Dear Staff,

Enclosed is a U.S. Postal Money Order in the amount of sixty ($60.00) dollars.

Also enclosed are a Original Promissory Note, a Share Certificate and Apostille certification documents. Along with a UCC-1 Financial Statement and a UCC-1 Security Agreement.

A portion of the funds are to be used for "Records and Registration of all enclosed documents.

As it regards additional funds, please use for next-day air service mailed back to me.

Your assistance in this matter is gratefully appreciated.

Sincerely,

STATE OF FLORIDA UNIFORM
COMMERCIAL CODE FINANCING STATEMENT FORM

A. NAME & DAYTIME PHONE NUMBER OF CONTACT PERSON
(Your contact information) "Direct"

B. SEND ACKNOWLEDGEMENT TO:

Name

Address

Address   **SELF EXPLANATORY**

City/State/Zip

THE ABOVE SPACE IS FOR FILING OFFICE USE ONLY

1. DEBTOR'S EXACT FULL LEGAL NAME — INSERT ONLY **ONE** DEBTOR NAME (**1a OR 1b**) – Do Not Abbreviate or Combine Names

1.a ORGANIZATION'S NAME	**NAME OF CORPORATION**			
1.b INDIVIDUAL'S LAST NAME		FIRST NAME	MIDDLE NAME	SUFFIX
1.c MAILING ADDRESS Line One **CORPORATION ADDRESS**		This space not available.		
MAILING ADDRESS Line Two	CITY	STATE **FLA.**	POSTAL CODE **Zip Code**	COUNTRY **U.S.**
1.d TAX ID# **EIN Number**	REQUIRED ADD'L INFO RE: ORGANIZATION DEBTOR	1.e TYPE OF ORGANIZATION **'C Corp.' or 'LLC'**	1.f JURISDICTION OF ORGANIZATION **FLA., GA., etc.**	1.g ORGANIZATIONAL ID# ☐ NONE

2. ADDITIONAL DEBTOR'S EXACT FULL LEGAL NAME — INSERT ONLY **ONE** DEBTOR NAME (**2a OR 2b**) – Do Not Abbreviate or Combine Names

2.a ORGANIZATION'S NAME	SAME NAME OF CORP. If OTHER PARTNERS ARE INVOLVED THEN COMPLETE 'ADDITIONAL DEBTOR'			
2.b INDIVIDUAL'S LAST NAME		FIRST NAME	MIDDLE NAME	SUFFIX
2.c MAILING ADDRESS Line One		This space not available.		
MAILING ADDRESS Line Two	CITY	STATE	POSTAL CODE	COUNTRY
2.d TAX ID#	REQUIRED ADD'L INFO RE: ORGANIZATION DEBTOR	2.e TYPE OF ORGANIZATION	2.f JURISDICTION OF ORGANIZATION	2.g ORGANIZATIONAL ID# ☐ NONE

3. SECURED PARTY'S NAME (or NAME of TOTAL ASSIGNEE of ASSIGNOR S/P) – INSERT ONLY **ONE** SECURED PARTY (**3a OR 3b**)

3.a ORGANIZATION'S NAME				
3.b INDIVIDUAL'S LAST NAME **YOUR INFORMATION** (in Personal Capacity)		FIRST NAME	MIDDLE NAME	SUFFIX
3.c MAILING ADDRESS Line One **ADDRESS**		This space not available.		
MAILING ADDRESS Line Two	CITY	STATE **GA.**	POSTAL CODE **Zip Code**	COUNTRY **U.S.**

4. This **FINANCING STATEMENT** covers the following collateral: In any Jurisdiction where the Uniform Commercial Code is in effect, (Name of Corp.) LLC, grants Your Personal Capacity, a security interest valued at One Million U.S. Dollars ($1,000,000.00); for a lien regarding the full cash amount, in exchange for an equal value in negotiated private property. The Secured Party is the Holder-in Due-course of this lien; and in case of default, accepts all accounts, notes, Inventory, intellectual properties, proceeds, goods, equipment and or interest in other business/property - currently and or herein after owned by said debtor above - located anywhere in the World. **SEE SECURITY AGREEMENT ATTACHED** This Financial Statement and Security Agreement takes 1st priority over any other demand against any other creditor, lender, investor, financial backer etc. whether by re-organization, merges, buy-outs, partnerships, shareholders, etc.; and should be immediately terminated upon fulfilling its obligations to Secured Party above.
This Financial Statement and Security Agreement shall become immediately effective at the moment of signing by both parties; and shall insure the responsibility of both signatory parties in accordance with the arranged Financial Statement/Security Agreement pursuant to UCC Statutes.

5. ALTERNATE DESIGNATION (if applicable) ☐ LESSEE/LESSOR ☐ CONSIGNEE/CONSIGNOR ☐ BAILEE/BAILOR
☐ AG. LIEN ☐ NON-UCC FILING ☐ SELLER/BUYER

6. Florida **DOCUMENTARY STAMP TAX** — YOU ARE REQUIRED TO CHECK **EXACTLY ONE** BOX

☐ All documentary stamps due and payable or to become due and payable pursuant to s. 201.22 F.S., have been paid.
☐ Florida Documentary Stamp Tax is not required.

7. OPTIONAL FILER REFERENCE DATA

STANDARD FORM - FORM UCC-1 (REV.01/2009)   Filing Office Copy   Approved by the Secretary of State, State of Florida

SECURING BUSINESS LOANS

Serial No. _____

GREEDY ENTERTAINMENT
COLLATERALIZED CORPORATE NONRECOURSE PROMISSORY NOTE

Amount: $1,000,000.00
One Million United States Dollars

Payee: Name of Note Holder

GREEDY Entertainment, having addressed at _____
__, FOR VALUE RECEIVED, hereby undertake to pay against the receipt of this Irrevocable, Transferable, Endorsable, Assignable, and Unconditional Nonrecourse Promissory Note, Payable against First Demand, to the Order of: _____(Name of Note Holder)_____ .

Terms: FIRST DEMAND
Currency: UNITED STATES
Issue Date: (SELL DATE OF INTELLECTUAL AND OTHER PROPERTY)
Maturity Date: FIRST DEMAND (or prior to the last day of the 5th year of the issue date)
Interest Rate: N/A

Default: IF ANY OF SAID PAYMENT UNDER THIS NOTE IS NOT PAID WHEN DUE, THE ENTIRE PRINCIPAL AMOUNT SHALL BE IMMEDIATELY DUE; AND SHALL PREVENT '**ANY**' OTHER INVESTOR, CREDITOR, LENDER, ETC. FROM RECEIVING '**ANY**' PAYMENT FROM THIS CORPORATION, PRIOR TO THE SATISFACTORY OF THIS NOTE.

Collateral: **INTELLECTUAL AND OTHER TANGIBLE PROPERTY**

Type of Issue: THIS PROMISSORY NOTE IS A SOLE PROMISSORY NOTE AUTHORIZED BY GREEDY ENTERTAINMENT, FOR THE PAYMENT AGAINST THE RECEIPT OF THIS IRREVOCABLE, TRANSFERABLE, ENDORSABLE, ASSIGNABLE, AND UNCONDITIONAL NONRECOURSE PROMISSORY NOTE.

IN WITNESS WHEREOF, GREEDY ENTERTAINMENT HAS CAUSED THIS PROMISSORY NOTE TO BE SIGNED ITS NAME BY ITS (TITLE OF OFFICER) AND WITNESSED AVAL BY A BANKING INSTITUTION; AND AFFIXING THE CORPORATE SEAL THIS _____DAY OF _____201_____.

_____
GREEDY ENTERTAINMENT (TITLE OF OFFICER)

_____
BANK OFFICER

_____   SEAL (OF GREEDY ENTERTAINMENT)
TITLE OF BANK OFFICER

_____
I.D. NUMBER OF BANK OFFICIAL   SEAL (OF BANK)

_____
PHONE NUMBER OF BANK

THIS IS A UCC-1 SECURITY AGREEMENT

Made by And Between

_____as Debtor

and

_____as Secured Party

Dated as of this _____day of_____201_____.

This Instrument Grants a Security Lien;

This Instrument is a Binding Agreement;

This Agreement Contains Future Advances Provisions;

and This Agreement Contains After-Acquired Property

TABLE OF CONTENTS

RECITALS 174

GRANTING CLAUSES

FIRST 175
SECOND 175
THIRD 176
FOURTH 176
EXCEPTED PROPERTY 176
IN THE EVENT OF DEFAULT 177
CURE OF LIABILITY/DEBT 177
HABENDUM 177

ARTICLE I

AGREEMENT DEEMED SECURITY AGREEMENT 178

ARTICLE II

AUTHORITY TO EXECUTE AND DELIVER NOTES 178

ARTICLE III

RECORDING AND REGISTERING NOTES & SECURITY AGREEMENT 178

ARTICLE IV

ORGANIZED RECORDS 178

ARTICLE V

SECURED PARTY RIGHT TO EXPEND MONEY 179

ARTICLE VI

LIMITATIONS ON TRANSFERS OF PROPERTIES 179

ARTICLE VII

EVENTS OF DEFAULTS 179

ARTICLE VIII
ATTORNEYS' FEES & OTHER COLLECTION COSTS *181*

ARTICLE IX
CURE OF LIABILITY/DEBT *181*

ARTICLE X
ASSIGNMENTS AND TRANSFERS OF NOTES *182*

ARTICLE XI
NOTICES *182*

ARTICLE XII
GOVERNING LAW *183*

ARTICLE XIII
EXECUTION OF PARTIES *183*

ARTICLE XIV
NOTARY *184*

UCC-1 **SECURITY AGREEMENT,** dated this _____day of _____201____; hereinafter called "agreement," is made by and between _____(hereinafter known as Debtor), a (Corp. or LLC) existing under the common laws of the State of _____; and (Your Full Name) (hereinafter known as Secured Party), a individual in his personal capacity.

RECITALS

WHEREAS, Debtor and Secured Party are the only parties to that certain **SECURITY AGREEMENT** dated as of this day of _____201____;

WHEREAS, Debtor deems it necessary to ACCEPT intellectual and other tangible personal property, for its Trust operations; and to issue its Promissory Notes and other debt obligations thereof from time to time in one or more series; and additionally agree to pledge its property hereinafter described or mentioned to secure payment of the same.

WHEREAS, Debtor decides to enter into this "agreement" pursuant to which all secured debt of the "agreement" hereunder shall be secured on parity.

WHEREAS, this "agreement" restates that priority of the lien shall secure the payment obligations under which indebtedness is described more particularly by listing the original notes is Schedule "A" hereto; and WHEREAS, all acts necessary to make this "agreement" a valid and binding legal instrument for the security of such notes and obligations, subject to the terms of this "agreement." have been in all respects duly authorized.

NOW THEREFORE, THIS AGREEMENT WITNESSETH: that to secure the property later described as intellectual and other tangible property and all property issued hereunder according to their tenor and effect, and the performance of all provisions therein and herein contained; and in consideration of the covenants herein contained, and the purchase or guarantee of notes by the guarantors or holders thereof, Debtor has agreed, pledged and granted a continuing security interest in, and by these presents does hereby grant, bargain, alienate, remise, release, convey, assign, transfer, hypothecate and grant a security interest and lien in for the purposes herein expressed, unto Secured Party all property, rights, privileges and franchises of Debtor, regarding every kind and description, whether real, personal or mixed, tangible and intangible, of the kind or nature specifically mentioned herein or ANY OTHER KIND OF NATURE (with the exception of EXCEPTED PROPERTY), now owned or hereafter acquired by Debtor, whether by purchase, consolidation, merger, donation, construction, erection or in any other way), wherever located in the world, including without limitation, all and singular the following:

GRANTING CLAUSE FIRST

a. All of those fee and leasehold interests in intellectual and other tangible Property set forth in Schedule "A" hereto, subject in each case to those matters set forth in such schedule;
b. All of Debtor's interests in the ownership of Properties described in the Schedule "A" attached, comprising any portions listed hereto, and any other after-acquired Properties;
c. All Property, rights, privileges allowances and franchises particularly described in either of the Schedule's annexes, which are hereby made part of, and deemed to be described in, this granting clause as fully as if set forth in this granting clause at length; and
d. All Property, real estate, lands, easements, servitudes, licenses, permits, allowances, consents, franchises, privileges and other rights in or relating to the Property obtained and attained, including structures, equipment, tools, furniture, etc.

GRANTING CLAUSE SECOND

All other Property, real, personal or mixed, of whatever kind and description and wheresoever situated, including without limitation, goods, accounts, money held in a Trust account pursuant hereto or to a "agreement" and general intangibles now owned or which may be hereafter acquired by

Debtor, but EXCLUDING EXCEPTED PROPERTY, now owned or which may be hereafter acquired by Debtor, it being the intention hereof that all property, rights, privileges, allowances and franchises now owned by Debtor or acquired by Debtor after the date hereof (other than excepted property) shall be as fully embraced within and subjected to the lien hereof as if such Property were specifically described herein.

GRANTING CLAUSE THIRD

Also any EXCEPTED Property that may, from time to time hereafter, by delivery or by writing of any kind, be subjected to the lien hereof by Debtor or by anyone in its behalf; and Secured Party is hereby authorized to receive the same at any time as additional security hereunder for the benefit of Secured Party. Such subjection to the lien hereof of any EXCEPTED Property as additional security may be made subject to any reservations, limitations, or conditions which shall be set forth in a written instrument executed by Debtor or the person so acting in its behalf or by such Secured Party respecting the use and disposition of such Property or the proceeds thereof.

GRANTING CLAUSE FOURTH

Together with all and singular the tenements, hereditaments and appurtenances belonging or in anywise appertaining to the aforesaid Property or any part thereof, with the reversion and reversions, remainder and remainders and all the tolls, earnings, rents, issues, profits, revenues, and other income, products and proceeds of the Properties subjected or required to be subjected to the lien of this "agreement;" in and to the same and every part thereof (other than EXCEPTED Property).

EXCEPTED PROPERTY

There is, however, expressly EXCEPTED and excluded from the lien and operation of this "agreement" the following described property of Debtor, now owned or hereafter acquired (and herein sometimes referred to as EXCEPTED Property).

Said EXCEPTED Property consist of twenty-five % (25%) of the remaining shares; and or twenty-five percent (25%) of the remaining company that owns said shares. The total twenty-five percent will include after acquired properties as well.

IN THE EVENT OF DEFAULT

PROVIDED, HOWEVER, that if, upon the occurrence of an "event of default" by Debtor, Secured Party may, to the extent permitted by law, at the same time likewise take possession thereof of all assets described in GRANTING CLAUSE FIRST, GRANTING CLAUSE SECOND, GRANTING CLAUSE THIRD and GRANTING CLAUSE FOURTH.

CURE OF LIABILITY/DEBT

Whenever all events of default shall have been cured or satisfied, then the possession of substantially all of the agreed Properties, titles and ownerships must be free of lien and be owned solely by Debtor.

HABENDUM

TO HAVE AND TO HOLD all said Properties, rights, privileges and franchises of every kind and descriptions, real, personal or mixed, hereby and hereafter granted, bargained, sold, alienated, remised, released, conveyed, assigned, transferred, agreed, encumbered, hypothecated, pledged, setover, confirmed or subjected to a continuing security interest and lien as aforesaid, together with all the appurtenances thereto appertaining (said Properties, rights, privileges and franchises, including any cash and securities hereafter deposited), being herein collectively called the agreed Properties, unto Secured Party and the respective assigns of Secured Party forever, to secure equally and ratably the payment of the principle on the notes, according to its terms, without preference, priority or distinction as to principle (except as otherwise specifically provided herein) or as to lien or otherwise of any note over and any other note by reason of the priority in time of execution, delivery or maturity thereof or of the assignment or negotiation thereof or otherwise, and to secure the due performance of all of the covenants, agreements and provisions herein and in the agreements contained; and for the uses and purposes and upon the terms, conditions, provisos and agreements hereinafter expressed and declared, and whether tangible or intangible.

ARTICLE I AGREEMENT DEEMED SECURITY AGREEMENT

To the extent that any of the Properties described or referred to in this "agreement" is Governed by the provisions of the Uniform Commercial Code (UCC); and this "agreement" is hereby deemed a "Security Agreement" under UCC.

ARTICLE II AUTHORITY TO EXECUTE AND DELIVER NOTES

Debtor is authorized under its its Trust Minutes and By-Laws to execute and deliver notes; and this Security Agreement is valid and enforceable in accordance with its respective terms.

ARTICLE III RECORDING AND REGISTERING NOTES & SECURITY AGREEMENT

Promptly after the execution and delivery of this instrument, it should be registered and filed to the extent necessary to make effective the lien intended to be created by this "agreement" and reciting the details stating that all agreements and financing statements have been executed, registered and recorded, that are necessary fully to preserve and protect the rights of Secured Party in compliance with this "agreement" including liens on any Properties acquired by Debtor after the execution and delivery of this Instrument; and that such further action has been taken with respect to the recording, registering and filing thereof.

ARTICLE IV ORGANIZED RECORDS

Debtor will keep proper books, records and accounts in which full and correct entries shall be made of all dealings or transactions of or in relation to the notes, Properties business and affairs of of Debtor. Debtor will additionally at any and all times, upon written request of Secured Party (but at the expense of Debtor), permit Secured Party or its representatives to inspect any books of accounts, Properties, agreed properties hereunder, after acquired properties, records, reports and other documents of Debtor; and to take copies of same and extracts therefrom. Debtor will also afford and procure a reasonable opportunity to make any such inspection, and all such information as Secured Party may request (including furnishings of such), with respect to the performance of Debtor of its covenants under this Security Agreement.

ARTICLE V SECURED PARTY RIGHT TO EXPEND MONEY

Secured Party may, in its sole discretion, advance funds in order to insure Debtor's compliance with this covenant, which indirectly preserves or protects any right of interest of Secured Party pursuant to this "agreement."

ARTICLE VI LIMITATIONS ON TRANSFERS OF PROPERTIES

Debtor must not, without the prior written approval of Secured Party, sell, or transfer any agreed Property hereunder to any other person, group, or entity.

ARTICLE VII EVENTS OF DEFAULT

a. Each of the following circumstances shall amount to an "event of default:"
1. A petition filed by or on behalf of Debtor in bakruptcy;
2. Be adjudicated a bankrupt or insolvents;
3. Make an assignment for the benefit of its creditors;
4. Consent to the appointment of a receiver for itself or of its Property;
5. Institute proceedings for its reorganization;
6. Proceedings instituted by others for its reorganization;
7. The forfeiture or deprivation of Debtor's corporate charter or franchises, permits, easements or licenses required to carry on any material portion of its business;
8. and or any material misrepresentation or warranty made by Debtor within this Security Agreement; or in any certificate of financial statement delivered hereunder or thereunder which shall prove to be false or misleading in any material respect at the time made.

b. If any of "the event of defaults" shall occur, Secured Party may personally, or use assistants to:

1. take immediate possession of the agreed Properties hereunder, collect and receive all credits, outstanding accounts and bills receivable of Debtor and all rents, income, revenues, proceeds and profits pertaining to or arising from the agreed properties and or any parts thereof, whether then past due or accruing thereafter, and issue binding receipts therefor; and manage control and operate the agreed Properties hereunder as fully as Debtor might due if in possession thereof, including, without limitation, the making of all repairs or replacements deemed necessary or advisable by Secured Party in possession;
2. Declare the principal of all its notes secured hereunder to be due and payable immediately by a notice in writing to Debtor; and failure of Debtor to provide said notice to Secured Party shall not affect the validity of any acceleration of the note or notes by Secured Party hereunder. And upon such Declaration by Secured Party, all unpaid principal (and premium, if any) shall become due and payable immediately;
3. Proceed to protect and enforce the rights of Secured Party by suits or actions in equity or at law in any court or courts of competent jurisdiction, whether for specific performance of any covenant or other agreement contained herein or in aid of the execution of any power herein granted or for the foreclosure hereof or hereunder or for the sale of the agreed Properties, or any part thereof, or to collect the debts hereby secured; or for the enforcement of such other or additional appropriate legal or equitable remedies as may be deemed necessary or advisable to protect and enforce the rights and remedies herein granted or conferred; and of all proceeds, rents, income, revenues and profits pertaining thereto or arising therefrom, whether then past due or accruing after the appointment of such receiver, derived, received or had from the time of the commencement of such suit or action, and such receiver shall have all the usual powers and duties of receivers in like and similar cases, to the fullest extent permitted by law;
4. Sell or cause to be sold all and singular agreed Properties or any part thereof, and all right, title, interest, claim and demand of Debtor therein and thereto, at public auction at such place in any county (or its equivalent locality) in which the Properties to be sold, or any part thereof, is located, at such time and upon such terms as may be specified in a notice of sale, which shall state the time when and the place where the sale is to be held;

and shall contain a brief general description of the Properties to be sold, and shall be given by mailing a copy thereof to the Debtor in at least fifteen (15) days prior to the date fixed for such sale and by publishing the same once in a week for two consecutive calendar weeks prior to the date of such sale in a newspaper or general circulation in such locality, the first such publication to be not less than fifteen (15) days (no more than thirty (30) days prior to the date fixed for such sale); and may be adjourned from time to time by announcement at the time and place appointed for such sale or for such adjourned sale or sales; and without further notice or publication the sale may be had at the time and place which the same shall be adjourned, PROVIDED, HOWEVER, that in the event another or different notice of sale or another or different manner of conducting the same shall be required by law, the notice of sale shall be given or the sale be conducted, as the case may be, in accordance with the applicable provisions of law. The expense incurred by Secured party (including, but not limited to, receiver's fees, counsel fees, cost of advertisements and agents compensations) in the exercise of any of the remedies provided in this Security Agreement shall be secured by this "agreement."

ARTICLE VIII ATTORNEYS' FEES & OTHER COLLECTION COSTS

In "the event of default" Debtor agrees to pay all of Secured Party's expenses actually incurred to enforce or collect any of the obligations including, without limitation, reasonable arbitration, paralegals, attorneys' and other experts' fees and expenses whether incurred without the commencement of a suit, in any trial, arbitration, or administration proceeding, or in any appellate or bankruptcy proceeding, banking expenses incurred to enforce or collect any of the Guaranteed obligations, including, without limitation, reasonable arbitration, paralegals' attorneys' experts and other fees and expenses, whether incurred without the commencement of a suit, in any suit, arbitration, or administration proceeding, or in any appellate or bankruptcy proceeding.

ARTICLE IX CURE OF LIABILITY/DEBT

If Debtor shall pay or cause to be paid, the whole amount of the Principal (and premium, if any) on the Promissory Note at the times and in the manners hereunder provided, and shall also pay or cause to be paid all other sums payable hereunder, then and in that case, all Properties and rights hereby conveyed, assigned, or pledged shall be free of lien and owned solely by Debtor and such attachments of Secured Party shall thereupon cease and become void; and Secured Party shall, upon the record, enter satisfaction of this "agreement" to all places wherein the Promissory Note, Properties, and agreement was recorded, registered and filed.

ARTICLE X ASSIGNMENTS AND TRANSFERS OF NOTES

At any given time, for any given reason, Secured Party may transfer the Promissory Notes and Security Agreement hereof, in whole, part and or portions, to any other person, entity group or individual (at any stage of debts by Debtor), at Secured Party's discretion. In such case, all provisions, clauses, and sections of this "agreement" shall apply to the New secured Patty whom such "agreement" is transferred to. Debtor shall have no say or discretion of how Secured Party reassigns and or transfer this Security Agreement, or its Promissory Note.

ARTICLE XI NOTICES

All demands, notices, reports, approvals, designations or directions required or permitted to be given hereunder shall be in writing and shall be deemed to be properly given if sent by registered or certified mail, postage prepaid; or delivered by hand and or sent by facsimile, transmission, receipt confirmed, addressed to the proper Party(s) at the following addresses:

As to Debtor:_____Debtor's name;
_____address;
_____City, State;
_____Zip Code

As to Secured Party_____Secured Party's Name;
_____address;
_____City, State;
_____Zip Code

Any such Party(s) may, from time to time, designate to each other a new address to which demands, notices, reports, approvals, designations or directions may be addressed; and from and after any such designation the address designated shall be deemed to be the address of such Party in lieu of the addresses given above.

ARTICLE XII GOVERNING LAW

This Security Agreement ("agreement") shall be construed in and Governed by the laws of Contract law; and the jurisdiction for any complaints, should any arise, shall be token within the State of _____, County of_____. Additionally, should any of this "agreement" is found to be inoperable according to law, then such part shall be stricken and the remainder of the "agreement" shall remain in effect.

ARTICLE XIII EXECUTION OF PARTIES

The signatures below BINDS both Parties to this "agreement" and the full terms herein.
WHEREFORE, IN WITNESS WHEREOF, Debtor has caused this SECURITY AGREEMENT to be signed in its name and stamped by its seal, to be hereunto affixed and attested by its officers thereunto duly authorized; all as of the day and year first written.
AND SECURED PARTY, has accepted as a truth, that all clauses, provisions, and terms therefor stated within this "agreement" is agreed to by free will, absent coercion, threat, intimidation, etc.

_____Debtor's Signature
_____Debtor's Title
_____Secured Party's Signature

STATE OF_____
COUNTY OF_____

On this_____day of_____201___, before me appeared_____as Debtor and _____as Secured Party, both having been duly sworn by me, did prove to me that one of them Represents Debtor and the other is Secured Party; and that the seal of Debtor is affixed to the foregoing Instrument is that indeed the seal of Debtor; and that this Instrument was signed and sealed on behalf of Debtor by Authority of its designation; and that both, Secured Party and Debtor acknowledged that the execution of said Instrument was a free act and deed of said Debtor.

IN WITNESS WHEREOF, I have hereunto, set my hand and official seal on this_____day of_____201_____.

_____

NOTARY

My Commission Expires:

SCHEDULE "A"

UCC-1 Security Agreement Attachment

The maximum debt obligated pursuant to this agreement has been agreed upon to consist of "one Million U.S. Dollars" ($1,000,000), in addition to _____% annual interest.

The agreed upon exchange of Property to be held in lien as collateral is:

1. Promissory Note;

2. UCC-1 Financial Statement;

3. UCC-1 Security Agreement; and

4. 750,000 shares of <u>Your Co. Name</u>_____, Inc. (or LLC)

When the loan is repaid, you would have to file the following document, informing all parties that the loan borrowed has been satisfied in full and that all collateral placed for the security of said loan shall be returned unliened. Be sure that a copy is filed with both, the county courthouse and your Secretary Department of State.

CERTIFICATION OF SATISFACTION

KNOW ALL BY THESE PRESENTS:

That **(name, title),** representing **(beneficiary),** does hereby certify and acknowledge, under penalties of perjury, that the **promissory note** or other evidence of indebtedness secured by that certain mortgage/deed of trust made by _____to ____ _____, mortgage/trustee(s), dated _____ and recorded _____ as Instrument No. _____ among the Land Records of the District of Columbia, which encumbers the real property described in Exhibit A attached hereto, has been fully paid and satisfied and that _____ _____ was, at the time of satisfaction, the holder of the **promissory note** or other evidence of indebtedness and that the lien of the said mortgage/deed of trust is hereby released.

The property encumbered by said mortgage/deed of trust is described as follows:

WITNESS the hand and seal of the party making this certification this _____ day of _____,_____.

(ACKNOWLEDGMENT)

(e) (1) If a **promissory note** is paid or satisfied in full, the holder shall, within 30 days after receipt of such payment or within 30 days after such satisfaction, execute, acknowledge, and deliver, or cause to be executed, acknowledged and delivered, to the person making such payment or causing such **promissory note** to be satisfied, one or more of the documents, instruments and affidavits, in one of the forms permitted by subsection (c) of this section, sufficient to release the deed of trust securing such **promissory note** as a lien against the real property described in the deed of trust.

(2) If a **promissory note** is paid or satisfied in part, and if by the terms of the **promissory note,** the deed of trust securing the **promissory note** or a separate agreement between the parties, the person making such partial payment or causing such partial satisfaction to be made is entitled to a release of a part of the real property encumbered by the lien of the deed of

trust, the holder of the **promissory note** shall comply with the provisions of subsection (c)(3) of this section in the same manner as if the **promissory note** were paid or satisfied in full, except that the release shall apply only to the part of the real property encumbered by the lien of the deed of trust which the holder is obligated, by the terms of the **promissory note,** the deed of trust or the separate agreement, to release on account of such partial payment or satisfaction.

(3) If a holder of a **promissory note** secured by a deed of trust fails to execute, acknowledge, and deliver, or cause to be executed, acknowledged, and delivered, the documents, instruments, or affidavits required to release the deed of trust, in whole or in part, within the time, and in the manner, required by paragraph (1) or (2) of this subsection, and if the holder's failure continues for more than 30 days after the holder receives a written request therefor from the person entitled to the release or such person's agent, then holder shall pay to the person entitled to the release a penalty in the amount of $50 per day, shall be liable to such person for all actual and consequential damages caused by the holder's failure timely to deliver or record the full or partial release, and shall pay or reimburse such person for all costs and expenses, including reasonable attorneys fees and disbursements, relating to or arising out of the enforcement of such person's rights under this section. The penalty of $50 per day shall be payable for the period beginning on and including the 31st day after the holder receives a written request for the release to, but not including, the day on which the holder delivers the executed and acknowledged documents, instruments or affidavits required to release the deed of trust.

(4) For purposes of this subsection, (i) a payment in the form of an electronic transfer of immediately available funds to an account in a commercial bank, a savings bank, a savings and loan association, a credit union or a similar financial institution shall be deemed to be made when the financial institution confirms receipt of the funds to the owners of the account, (ii) a payment in the form of a check issued or certified by a national or state bank shall be deemed to be made upon receipt of the check, and (iii) payment in the form of a check that is not issued or certified by a national or state bank shall be deemed to be made on the first day on which the holder

receives the proceeds of collection of such check in immediately available funds.

(f) If a deed of trust is released, or deemed released, as a lien on all of the real property described therein, the release of the deed of trust shall be deemed automatically to release any ancillary security instrument that secures the same **promissory note** secured by the deed of trust. This provision shall not apply if the document recorded among the land records expressly states that the release of the deed of trust shall not release the ancillary security instrument.

FORM OF RELEASE AFFIDAVIT

FOR LOST, MISPLACED, OR DESTROYED **PROMISSORY NOTE** PER § 45-721(C)(1) [see now § 42-1101(3)(A)]:

KNOW ALL MEN BY THESE PRESENTS:
THAT I, the undersigned, hereby certify under penalties of perjury that:

1. I was the last known holder of a certain **promissory note** (or the trustees named in the original deed of trust or substitute trustees appointed by an instrument of substitution recorded in the land records);

2. Despite diligent search, I have been unable to locate the original **promissory note** which has been lost, misplaced or destroyed, (if the holder add: and neither the **promissory note** nor any interest therein has been transferred, assigned or negotiated to any other person);

3. The **promissory note** has been fully paid and satisfied; and

4. The deed of trust dated **(date)** securing said **promissory note** granted by **(grantor)** in favor of **(trustee(s))** securing **(grantee)** and recorded in the land records on **(date)** in Liber _____, at Folio _____, as instrument no. _____ and constituting a lien upon that piece or parcel of land located in the District of Columbia and known as:

LOT _____ in SQUARE _____, (additional legal description, ex. subdivision) as per plat recorded in Liber _____ at Folio _____ among the land records is hereby RELEASED.

WITNESS the hand and seal of the undersigned **[noteholder/trustee/substitute trustee]** this _____ day of _____, _____.

STATE/DISTRICT of _____)
) ss:
COUNTY of _____)
I, the undersigned, a Notary Public in and for the aforesaid do hereby certify that _____ party to and who is personally well known to me as the person who executed the foregoing Release Affidavit dated the _____ day of _____, _____, personally appeared before me in said jurisdiction and acknowledged the same to be his/her/its act and deed.

Given under my hand and seal, this _____ day of _____, and:

My commission expires:

_____
Notary Public

FORM OF RELEASE AFFIDAVIT

TO ACCOMPANY **PROMISSORY NOTE** § 45-721(2) [see now § 42-1101(3) (B)] : KNOW ALL MEN BY THESE PRESENTS:
THAT I, the undersigned, hereby certify under penalties of perjury that:
1. I am [the last known holder of the attached **promissory note** marked ["Paid" or "canceled"] or [an officer of the undersigned title insurance company] or [a validly licensed title insurance agent] which disbursed funds in payment of the **promissory note;**
2. the attached **promissory note** has been fully paid, canceled or satisfied; and

3. the deed of trust dated **(date)** securing said **promissory note** granted by **(grantor)** in favor of **(trustees)** securing **(grantee)** and recorded in the Land Records on **(date)** in Liber _____, at Folio _____, as instrument no. _____ and constituting a lien upon that piece or parcel of land located in the District of Columbia and known as:

LOT _____ in SQUARE _____, (additional legal description, ex. subdivision) as per plat recorded in Liber _____ at Folio _____ among the Land Records is hereby RELEASED.

WITNESS the hand and seal of the undersigned **[noteholder/trustee/ substitute trustee]** this _____ day of _____, _____.

STATE/DISTRICT of _____)
) ss:
COUNTY of _____)

I, the undersigned, a Notary Public in and for the aforesaid do hereby certify that _____ party to and who is personally well known to me as the person who executed the foregoing Release Affidavit dated the _____ day of _____, _____, personally appeared before me in said jurisdiction and acknowledged the same to be his/her/its act and deed.

Given under my hand and seal, this _____ day of _____, and:

My commission expires:

_____
Notary Public.

CHAPTER 13
UNTAPPED COMMERCIAL ACCOUNTS

In your beginning stages you're going to need to acquire all of the office and other necessities you need, while trying to spend as less as possible. At this juncture everything counts and a penny saved is a penny earned. Unnecessarily spent money deprives your company from seeing a profit earlier than one is made.

Few people operating businesses fail to realize that everything don't require a loan or a credit card borrowing; and yet, your goods, materials, and services can still be acquired, all in the name of consignment. This is called "Business to Business Dealing" (B2B) or securing commercial accounts.

Under either of the above terms, transactions takes place in the form of vendor trade credit, which is beneficial to both you and the vendor. Here's how this kinda works or plays out:

A vendor orders his or her inventory. That inventory is designed to be sold under any or whatever circumstances there is, without losing its minimum value. Now many of these products will be sold, but all of them:must go because new products are introduced everyday.

So when a customer applies for a commercial account and is approved; and ultimately needs a product, the vendor has just relieved itself of a product that is almost guaranteed the price it sought to sell it for. Because regardless if the product is paid for or not, the vendor can write it off as a company loss. If the customer pays, then the vendor knows that it has made a great decision in choosing a responsible customer; and whenever the customer shops, the vendor knows that a certain amount of their products can be sold with minimum risk.

Sooner than later, the vendor will be contacting the customer, in an effort to unload products onto him or her, without the customer inquiring. This is credit building at its finest.

Sometimes, companies are grown from the ground up in this manner, because customers themselves have buyers in place; and in turn, they're making a profit off of a product that they never spent one dime on.
Payment terms varies from vendor to vendor, many of which requires two different terms: 'Net 30' and 'Net 60.' Lets look at them closely.

Net 30:
Net 30 represents the number of days the customer has to pay back the vendor for the products they were credited. The maximum time allowed to pay-n-full is 30 days.

Net 60:
Gives the customer 60 days to pay back the vendor in full.

There is normally no interest charge if the payments are timely paid-in-full. But if a customer goes beyond the maximum time allowed, then a interest rate is arbitrarily fixed, as long as it doesn't violate federal or state usury laws.

But forget all this, you wanna know how you can get some straight cash out of these accounts. It's simple, but keep this on the low too or else the companies will change its uses.
First thing you wanna do is when you open your bank account, to secure a merchant account at the same time. What you'll get is a credit card reader, that allows companies and others to pay for your products by credit cards. It is one of the biggest methods of payment today. Well, you can purchase store gift cards with your commercial accounts and then swipe those gift cards onto your merchant account and the money would go direct deposit into your company bank account. And there you have it....cash money.
But this is only if you're in desperate need of money and you don't have any at your disposal at the time. Securing commercial accounts, which is no more than store credit cards, is one of the vital ways of staying in business. Every commercial store offers a store credit card and it takes only seconds to fill out the questionnaire. Companies are almost always approved. And you can apply at unlimited different stores for them. Use them. Its free money.

CHAPTER 14
USING YOUR OWN MONEY AS LEVERAGE

Using the money that you do have, as leverage is a wonderful tactic that has proved lucrative throughout time. For example, there was once upon a time that you could get almost 90% more value for using your actual money, than you could have never gotten if you didn't have a dime. Today however, the value is much lower, although it still provides nearly 70% of your actual on-hand money. The lucrative part that comes into play is when that of which you purchase, appreciates.

In this tactic you are able to do more with less....much less. Nearly all loans are approved when the loan applicant has their own money that they are willing to include in the project they're seeking the loan for. This helps loan officers and financial institutions in determining how much belief that the sought borrower, believes in the project being a likely success. So whatever you do, utilize the benefit of using your own money to secure a worth of at least a minimum of 70% of its value.

LEGALLY CHANGE YOUR NAME TO A NAME THAT EXHUDES MONEY, POWER AND RESPECT

None of us can help the names that our mothers, fathers, aunts, uncles, step parents, adopted parents, guardians, etc. gave us. Some of us may like them because they sound cool, hip, fancy, famous, etc.; and then some of us may not because neither of them don't.

Some are so common or plain until we move to change them ourselves. Then some of the names we're given are disliked by us because they just don't fit us at all.

This chapter allows us to take control of our namesake and change it to whatever we think fits us most. And this could be whatever we come up with to change it to. After all, nobody told us that we're automatically Granted this right when we turn 18.

However, your name should not just be a common name, it should represent so much more. It should be well thought out, at least at a minimum of 6 months before you decide on it. And it should represent money, power and respect. Overall, it should fit, because we all know that red flags arise when a person's name don't fit. For example, what is a black man's legal name doing being Tong Wong? Or a white man's legal name Reggie Black? Or a Chinese man's legal name William Johnson?

Hereinafter is a motion for you to fill in and file with your county courthouse. All that is required is a court filing fee, which shouldn't cost move than $150.00. When you get your order back from the court Granting your legal name change, then you can immediately began using it. There are however a few things that should be done though:
1. Immediately visit the DMV (Division of Motor Vehicles) and make the change in your driver's license;

2. Visit your Social Security Office and make the name change on your social security card;

3. And visit your Vital Statistic Office and make the name change on your birth certificate.

CAUTION: Don't make any changes in your home address or bills because then it may show up in a database, that you have changed your name to the new name that you will be living in; and you don't want that because if that happens then you have defeated the purpose of re-inventing yourself. Remember, the name change separates you from the old person. The objective is to always shift, camouflage, hide, and suppress the connection. **REMEMBER,** you are to **NEVER** use your old name again in your life. Consider that person no longer in existence. You have to become a new person. Believe and mean it with all of your heart. If you don't, you'll show up in a google database with different alias'.

IN THE CIRCUIT COURT
_____ JUDICIAL DISTRICT
IN AND FOR _____ COUNTY

IN RE: THE NAME CHANGE OF

_____,
Petitioner

Case No._____
Division._____

PETITION FOR ADULT CHANGE OF NAME
PURSUANT TO _____ STATE _____ STATUTES

COMES NOW, _____, date of birth _____, Social Security No. _____, being Duly Sworn, HEREBY CERTIFY, that the following information is true and correct for purposes of this name change request:

1. That the above styled name is my full and complete legal name given at birth and recorded in hospital and vital statistics records;

2. That the above styled legal name be legally changed to _____;

3. That I was born In the County of _____, within the State of _____; within the country of _____ _____;

4. That my father's full legal name and identity is _____ _____;

5. That my mother's full legal name and identity is

6. That if my mother was ever married, that her maiden name is_____;

7. That I have lived at the following addresses:

a.
b.
c.
d.
e.
f.
g.
h.

8. That I have _____**Never or** _____**Been** married;

9. That the full legal names, date of births and social security numbers of each of my children are:

a.

b.

c.

d.

e.

f.

LEGALLY CHANGE YOUR NAME TO A NAME THAT EXHUDES MONEY, POWER AND RESPECT

10. That my name have never been legally changed before by a court of law;

11. That I have never been known or called by any other names except said name recorded by vital statistics;

12. That I ___**do or** ___**do not** operate a business;

13. That I have obtained a high school diploma or G.E.D. from _____, on _____;

14. That my past arrests consists of: _____Nothing, or

a.
b.
c.
d.
e.
f.
g.

15. That I have or never have been declared or adjudicated bankrupt;

16. That I have or never had a monetary judgement entered against me by a court, on behalf of a creditor;

17. That I have no ulterior or illegal motive and nor purpose, for filing this petition; and granting it will not in any manner invade the property rights of others, whether partnership, patent, good will, privacy, copyright, trademark or otherwise.

I understand that I am swearing or affirming under oath to the truthfulness of the claims made in this petition, and that the punishment for knowingly making a false statement includes fines and or Imprisonment.

Executed on this _____ day of _____201___.

_____
Your Name

STATE OF_____
COUNTY OF_____

Before Me was _____, whom executed the foregoing signature on this _____ day of _____, 201_____;
and whom produced legal and or lawful identification proving such; and I have witnessed said signature as a notary with the state of _____, County of _____, on this _____ day of _____, 201___.

                                                                                                        _____
                                                                                                                                     Notary

My Commission Expires:

CHAPTER 16
BURYING NEGATIVE INFORMATION ABOUT YOU ON GOOGLE

In today's world, you can find out just about anything on anybody on Google. This is what the world needed, when it regarded the research about one's background when the information is needed for the decision making on much serious matters. I mean, people do wanna ultimately know that they're not dealing with serial killers and rapists, and everything else that is considered to be immorally wrong.

Google arrived on America's (and countries abroad) top favorite pick list when it introduced and provided this feature to the world. Google won over multi billions more people when it allowed anyone to upload positive or negative information that is known about an individual or individuals. Unfortunately though, Google don't sift through the countless uploads and determine which information is true or false; and as a detriment, malicious and slandering type people with ill intent in their hearts uploads millions of untrue, false, negative, shameful, and frightening things about a person that has not an single ounce of truth in it. Even creditors do it.

But I'm going to show you how to take your life back and bury all that negative info that someone has wasted time to upload on you. The process is simple as a,b,c.

1. First, find any and all sorts of publications that is talking about a whole bunch of nothing. Newspapers will do fine as well. Just be sure that none of the articles are from the Metro section.

2. Purchase a USB thumbdrive with a total of 10 gigabites of space; or a few USBs that equates to 10 gigabites of space; and fill them with the newspaper articles or content in the publications. You can even do both.

3. Then go on Google, pull up the individual name or names, and go into the section that allows you to upload information; then fill it with all 10 gigabites of information.

4. One week later, reload the USB thumbdrives with 10 more gigabites and do the same thing. But make sure when U reload the 10 gigabites of space, that you fill it with different content.

5. Repeat these steps for four weeks in a row and nobody on God's green earth will want to sit and read through all of that nonsense, while searching to find anything negative about you.

Some companies may charge you a fee to do this. But its not worth paying them when you can simply do it yourself and make sure its done. Besides, the fees that are charged are ridiculous.

Conclusion

Well, our journey along this yellow brick road has come to an end. I'm hopeful that you have paid grave attention and expanded your horizon as you have reached this point. The sky is the limit with this stuff and I can go on and on. However, it would cost you dearly. The most important things I wanted you to take from this material, is the fact that everything within is a lesson that you will learn from no school. So don't expect anyone to speak to you regarding any of these things, unless you know exactly what you are talking about; and trust me, they will drill you. Even then, they will only limit you to know some of what they know. They themselves will have already been working on a brilliance of ideas, regarding this knowledge. So choose your company wisely, because those that can't get any of this done will be quick to dispute that any of this is possible.

Also, don't concern yourself if you're not from Florida, I just only used said State as an example. Its safe to insert your own state where it applies. This knowledge is universal all over the United States. Welcome….to your life changing effects.

Index

A

Apostille letter 165, 167, 168
Author's Signature 12

B

Bank Resolution Letter 101, 112, 164
Board of Directors 89, 91, 94, 95, 99
Business Credit 163
Business loan 149

C

C' Corporation 101
C' Corporation form 101
Certification of Satisfication 185
Chairman 87
Collateral 84, 99, 119, 151, 152, 153, 154, 156, 157, 159, 160, 161, 163, 166, 169, 170, 184
Commercial Account 137, 190
Corporate Kit 112, 113
Corporations 54, 57, 63, 64, 77, 78, 80, 81, 83, 85, 86, 87, 91, 93, 102, 103, 104, 107, 108, 109, 112, 116, 117, 123, 141
Copyright Address 14
Copyright Board 12
Copyright Fees 14
Copyright forms 14
Copyright Notice 15, 21, 27, 33
Copyrights 8, 12, 14, 20, 26, 32, 38, 39, 2, 54, 112, 113, 150, 163
Credit Bureau 123, 135, 139, 145
Credit Bureau Form 123, 135, 139, 145
Credit Bureau Letters 123, 135, 139, 145
Credit Cards 14, 69, 74, 134, 138, 141, 191

Credit Lines 125, 134, 136, 137, 138, 140
Credit Limit 135, 139
Credit Rating 136, 137
Credit Report 121, 123, 124, 135, 142, 143, 144, 145, 146, 147

D

Digital Images 45
Domain Names 71, 72, 73, 74, 75, 112
Dun & Bradstreet 123, 124, 125, 132, 135, 136, 137
Dun & Bradstreet Questionaire 123, 124, 125, 132, 135, 136, 137
Duration of Trademark/Service Mark 41

E

EIN Number 111, 112, 113, 132, 137, 150, 154
Employee Agreement 95, 96
Employee Laws 96

F

Fictions Names 27
First Use 10, 39, 40, 41, 42, 44

I

Independent Contractor 96, 164
Infringement 13, 41, 102, 107
Infringement Fees 12, 41, 47
Irs. gov 89
Internal Revenue Services (IRS) 89

L

Lahman ACT
Library of Congress 2, 9, 10, 13, 14, 20, 21, 32, 42, 163
Limited Liability 64, 88, 93, 98, 100, 102, 103, 105, 114
List of Goods 43

LLC 174, 184
LLC Form 174, 184

M

Managing Member 95, 101, 102, 106, 119
Member Managed 95
Micro loan 166
Motion Mark 45

N

Name Change Form 194
Net 30 (TERMS) 30, 191
Net 60 (TERMS) 60, 191

P

Patent 33, 41, 42, 43, 58, 68, 69, 70, 196
Paydex Score 135, 136
Poor Man's Proof 42
Promissory Note 174, 181, 182, 184, 185, 186, 187, 188
Pseudonymous 12, 28

R

Rating 135, 136, 140
Records and Registration Letter 168
Registered Agent 99, 100, 102, 103, 105, 106, 108

S

SBA Express Loan 166
Secretary of State 76, 77, 78, 79, 80, 81, 82, 83, 84, 85, 86, 89, 97, 99, 169
Security Agreement 179, 181, 182, 183, 184
Service Mark 40, 41, 44, 47, 55, 56, 57, 62, 100
Shareholder 91, 95, 119, 124
Sound Recording Notice 10

Specimen 13, 42, 43, 44, 46
SS-4 Form 112, 113, 114
State Trademark Form 163
State Trademarks 54

T

Trademark 33, 39, 40, 41, 44, 46, 47, 54, 55, 56, 57, 62, 68, 73, 196
Trademark Infringement Fees 64, 65, 67
Trademark/Service Mark Fees 41, 42, 43, 58, 69, 70

U

UCC-1 Financial Statement Form 171, 174, 184
UCC-3 Financial Statement Form 155, 156
Uniform Commercial Code (UCC) 178

W

Www.whois.com 7 a Loan 72

Other Books
by David Dipoali

Smart Is The New Gangster: The Successful Record Label Guide

ISBN Number: 978-0-9903853-6-3;   978-0-9903853-7-0; and 978-0-9903853-8-7
                (book)   (E-book)   (MOBI)

'X' Marks The Spot: The Book of Entertainment Contracts

ISBN Number: 978-0-9903853-3-2;   978-0-9903853-4-9; and 978-0-9903853-5-6
                (book)   (E-book)   (MOBI)

www.ingramcontent.com/pod-product-compliance
Lightning Source LLC
Chambersburg PA
CBHW081815300426
44116CB00014B/2365